The Easter Rising

The Easter Rising

Revolution and Irish Nationalism

Second Edition

Alan J. Ward
The College of William and Mary

WILEY

This edition first published 2003.
© 2003 Harlan Davidson, Inc.

Harlan Davidson, Inc. was acquired by John Wiley & Sons in May 2012.

Registered Office
John Wiley & Sons, Ltd, The Atrium, Southern Gate, Chichester, West Sussex,
PO19 8SQ, UK

Editorial Offices
350 Main Street, Malden, MA 02148-5020, USA
9600 Garsington Road, Oxford, OX4 2DQ, UK
The Atrium, Southern Gate, Chichester, West Sussex, PO19 8SQ, UK

For details of our global editorial offices, for customer services, and for information
about how to apply for permission to reuse the copyright material in this book
please see our website at www.wiley.com/wiley-blackwell.

The right of Alan J. Ward to be identified as the author of this work has been
asserted in accordance with the UK Copyright, Designs and Patents Act 1988.

Library of Congress Cataloging-in-Publication Data
Ward, Alan J.
    The Easter Rising : revolution and Irish nationalism / Alan J. Ward—2nd. ed.
      p. cm.
    Includes bibliographical references and index.
    ISBN 978-0-882-95974-0 (alk. paper)
    1. Ireland—History—Easter Rising, 1916.   2. Ireland—Politics and government,
1910–1921. 3. Nationalism—Ireland—History—20th century. I. Title
    DA962 .W33 2003
    941.5082′1—dc21

                                              2002014594

Cover photo: Damage caused by the 1916 Easter Rising in Dublin. At right is the
O'Connell Bridge continuing into O'Connell Street with the O'Connell monument
at left, and the ruined areas around the Eden Quay. *Ap/Wide World Photos.*
Cover design: DePinto Graphic Design

Contents

Preface

THIS IS A SUBSTANTIALLY REVISED VERSION OF A BOOK I PUBlished in 1980. I was prompted to write the original by the fact that Irish nationalists and the British Army had been fighting each other for ten years in Northern Ireland. Because of that conflict I wanted to consider the troubled history of British-Irish relations, and the Rising provided a window through which I could approach the subject. It allowed me to explore some very important themes in Irish history without pretending to write a comprehensive history. In particular, I could write about nationalism in its various Irish forms and enter into the debate about the role of revolutionary violence in Ireland that the controversy in the north had reopened. By asking why the Rising occurred and what its effects have been I thought I could throw some light on the subject.

The Northern Ireland conflict was still not finally resolved when the century ended, twenty years after the book was published, which perhaps explains why there was still some demand for it. But by then the book was dated. If the book were to continue to be sold, I decided it should be rewritten. Twenty years of scholarship had to be incorporated to keep the book relevant, and it was also clear that the final chapter, on the effects of the Rising, required extensive revision because of the changes we have seen in Ireland, north and south.

As before, I drew heavily on my own research for this revision, including my book, *The Irish Constitutional Tradition: Responsible Government and Modern Ireland, 1782 to 1992* (Washington, DC, and Dublin, 1994), and the substantial literature that exists on this subject, which I have tried to acknowledge in the bibliography. I continue to be indebted to friends and colleagues in Irish studies, in Ireland and the United States, for their support over the years, and to the College of William and Mary for its generous support of my research and writing.

Alan J. Ward
Government Department
The College of William and Mary
Williamsburg, Virginia

CHAPTER 1

The Easter Rising

THIS IS A BOOK ABOUT THE CAUSES AND EFFECTS OF THE 1916 Easter Rising in Dublin, when a group of Irish nationalists sought to declare Ireland independent of the United Kingdom. The first task is to discover something about the Rising itself. What actually happened in Dublin in Easter Week, 1916, that was to change the course of Irish history?

April 24, 1916, was Easter Monday, and Dubliners were enjoying a public holiday. Many had left the city for the Fairyhouse races, and others were visiting the Royal Dublin Society Show. The weather was fine and the atmosphere relaxed when, at midday, peace was shattered by a rebellion in the city. Six days later portions of Dublin lay in ruins, hundreds were homeless, factories and shops were closed, one hundred thousand people (a third of the population) were on public relief, hundreds had died, and thousands were wounded.

The leaders of this rebellion might easily have been arrested long before it occurred. Although United Kingdom citizens at the time, they had been conducting a campaign against army recruiting in Ireland since World War I began in 1914, with antiwar newspapers, pamphlets, posters, and demonstrations. The Irish, they insisted, should not fight for the freedom of others until Ireland itself was free from British rule. Those who participated in the rebellion had been drilling openly and parading in Ireland with rifles and other weapons since the beginning of the war.

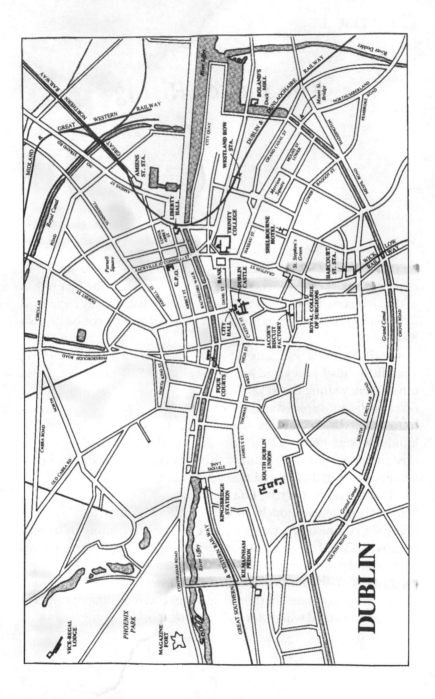

The overt dissidents were a small minority in a country which had supplied thousands of volunteers for the army, but the government treated them with considerable caution in the years leading up to 1916. Some antiwar activists were deported to Britain, and seditious newspapers were banned, but the minister responsible for Ireland, the Irish chief secretary, Augustine Birrell, opposed any systematic suppression of dissidents. He feared that it would precipitate an Irish crisis that would weaken the overall war effort. The Irish could argue that they were serving a higher Irish patriotism by refusing to be conscripted to fight in Europe, and their protests might arouse the latent antipathy to Britain that had long existed in Ireland. For this reason Ireland was excluded from conscription when it was introduced into Britain in January 1916. The government concluded that so long as Ireland supplied volunteers for the army, food for industrial Britain, and workers for British factories and farms, and so long as the antiwar dissidents were few in number, there would be no conscription and little repression.

By Easter 1916, however, the dissidents, known by the government and the general public as "Sinn Feiners," had gone too far. Rumors had flourished in Dublin for some time that a rebellion was being planned, and two events on Easter Saturday confirmed this suspicion. First, the navy captured a disguised German merchant ship carrying weapons and ammunition to the rebels. Its captain scuttled the ship at Queenstown, now Cobh, just outside Cork in the south of Ireland. Second, Sir Roger Casement, a retired British diplomat who had turned Irish revolutionary and had been recruiting a brigade to fight against England from Irish prisoners of war in Germany, was captured from a German submarine soon after landing in Tralee Bay, in the southwest of Ireland. The government immediately assumed that these events signified a treasonous conspiracy between Irish rebels and the United Kingdom's World War I enemy, Germany.

A German conspiracy was clearly intolerable, and Lord Wimborne, the lord lieutenant of Ireland, and Sir Matthew Nathan, the Irish under secretary and head of the Irish administration, cabled the chief secretary in London for permission to arrest the Sinn Fein leaders. They were too late. Nathan was in Dublin Castle, the headquarters of the

Irish administration, planning the arrests and awaiting permission to act, when the first shots were fired in the Easter Rising, on April 24, and the castle itself came under fire.

Despite the concerns of Wimborne and Nathan that a rebellion was likely, Dublin was totally unprepared for what happened that morning. The holiday was a completely normal one. General Friend, the commander in chief in Ireland, was in London on leave, and of the twenty-four hundred soldiers stationed in the city, only four hundred were on duty. At midday, the commander in chief of the Irish republican forces, Patrick Pearse, and his deputy, James Connolly, led their volunteers into action from Liberty Hall, the Irish Transport and General Workers' Union headquarters, just north of the River Liffey in central Dublin. Simultaneously, other republicans moved to prearranged sites around the city. One small group overpowered the single sentry on duty outside the Phoenix Park Magazine Fort and the eleven men stationed inside. The attackers carried away some arms and ammunition and blew up a small arms store, but they could not destroy the main store because the officer in charge had taken the key with him to the races. As a result, the great bang meant to signal the beginning of the Rising was only a whimper.

The republican army was an absurdly small group for a rebellion. The original plans for the Rising called for up to five thousand men to move in Dublin and thousands more throughout the country, perhaps as many as ten thousand in all. The leaders had hoped for a supply of German arms, and even at one time a German support force, but the Germans sent no troops, and their weapons were sunk in the waters off Queenstown. Furthermore, because of a leadership dispute and conflicting instructions, only about eight hundred volunteers obeyed the order to assemble in Dublin on Easter Monday. Others joined in during the week, but it is unlikely that more than fifteen hundred armed republicans were involved in all. They were supported by cooks and nurses from the Cumann na mBan, a republican women's organization, and by messengers from Fianna Éireann, a republican boy-scout organization, but the republicans mustered only about one-fourth of their anticipated strength. Nevertheless, the Rising lasted six days. The famous Irish rebellion of 1803, led by Robert Emmet, had lasted only one evening.

The republicans presented a rather incongruous sight. Some wore the uniforms of an organization known as the Irish Volunteers and others the uniforms of the two-hundred-strong Irish Citizen Army, which was the militia of the Irish Transport and General Workers' Union. The majority wore only military belts over civilian clothes. Their weapons were even more diverse than their garb. This is how one author described them: "The resistive appliances unwrapped on that Monday morning were a quartermaster's nightmare. . . . The rifles started with Sniders from old God's time and formed a chronology of arms-through-the-ages."[1] The republicans took shotguns, rifles, pistols of every gauge, grenades, and homemade bombs to face the British army.

In 1803, Emmet planned to capture Dublin Castle, and failed. The 1916 republicans could easily have succeeded because the small group that attacked the castle at about noon found only one member of the police on duty at the gate, whom they killed, and six soldiers in the guard room, whom they surprised and overpowered. Another twenty-five soldiers were in the castle garrison nearby but none stood between the attackers and Sir Matthew Nathan, who was in the main body of the castle. Had the attacking force been at full strength, or had they even anticipated such a light guard, both Dublin Castle and the Irish under secretary could have been seized in the opening minutes of the Rising. Instead, the rebels retreated to surrounding buildings, including the Dublin City Hall, from which they were flushed out by army fire on Tuesday.

The capture of the castle was just one example of the ease with which major buildings in the city could be taken. The Phoenix Park Magazine Fort was captured handily as well. The first battalion of the Dublin brigade of the republican forces, under Commandant Edward Daly, quickly occupied the Four Courts, home of the Irish judiciary, on the north bank of the River Liffey in the heart of the city. Although surrounding buildings and streets, particularly North King Street, were the scene of savage fighting, the Four Courts building was held by the rebels until they surrendered the following Saturday. To the west of the inner city, the South Dublin Union, a fifty-two acre workhouse, and some surrounding buildings were taken by 120 republicans of the fourth battalion under Commandant Eamonn Ceannt. Despite heavy fighting at close quarters, these were held until Sunday.

The bulk of the Irish Citizen Army, under Commandant Michael Mallin and his second-in-command, Countess Constance Markiewicz, the extraordinary Irish wife of a Polish count, occupied St. Stephen's Green, a large square south of the Liffey. They came under heavy British machine-gun fire on Tuesday morning from the Shelbourne Hotel, on the north side of the square and were forced to retreat to the College of Surgeons, on the western side. There they held out until Sunday, though very short of food. A little to the west of St. Stephen's Green was Jacob's Biscuit Factory, a stronghold which saw no major fighting and was occupied until Sunday by 150 of the second battalion under Commandant Thomas MacDonagh. To the east of the central city, 130 of the third battalion under Commandant Eamon de Valera occupied Boland's Flour Mill, and these, too, surrendered on Sunday.

The heaviest fighting of the Rising occurred at the Mount Street Bridge, south of the central city, where seventeen republicans occupied Clanwilliam House and other buildings covering a bridge over the Grand Canal. This was the route taken into Dublin on Wednesday morning by a thousand British reinforcements who had landed at the port of Kingstown, now Dun Laoghaire, six miles south of Dublin, the previous night. Over two hundred soldiers were killed or wounded before the handful of surviving republicans retreated from machine-gun fire and overwhelming numbers.

Mount Street Bridge and North King Street, near the Four Courts, saw the heaviest battles of the Rising, and there was heavy fighting both at the South Dublin Union and around Dublin Castle, but the symbolic heart of the Rising was the General Post Office (GPO) building on what was then Sackville Street, the main street in Dublin. It runs north of the O'Connell Bridge on the Liffey and is now O'Connell Street.

When Pearse and Connolly left Liberty Hall at midday on Easter Monday they marched with approximately 150 volunteers to the GPO, a few hundred yards away. They stormed into the building and overpowered the unarmed guard of seven. Shortly afterwards, Pearse appeared at the front of the building to read the Proclamation of the Irish Republic.

THE PROCLAMATION OF THE IRISH REPUBLIC (1916)
Poblacht na h-Éireann
The Provisional Government
of the
IRISH REPUBLIC
To the people of Ireland

Irishmen and Irishwomen: In the name of God and of the dead generations from which she receives her old tradition of nationhood, Ireland, through us, summons her children to her flag and strikes for her freedom.

Having organised and trained her manhood through her secret revolutionary organisation, the Irish Republican Brotherhood, and through her open military organizations, the Irish Volunteers and the Irish Citizen Army, having patiently perfected her discipline, having resolutely waited for the right moment to reveal itself, she now seizes that moment, and, supported by her exiled children in America and by gallant allies in Europe, but relying in the first on her own strength, she strikes in full confidence of victory.

We declare the right of the people of Ireland to the ownership of Ireland, and to the unfettered control of Irish destinies, to be sovereign and indefeasible. The long usurpation of that right by a foreign people and government has not extinguished the right, nor can it ever be extinguished except by the destruction of the Irish people. In every generation the Irish people have asserted their right to national freedom and sovereignty; six times during the past three hundred years they have asserted it in arms. Standing on that fundamental right and again asserting it in arms in the face of the world, we hereby proclaim the Irish Republic as a Sovereign Independent State, and we pledge our lives and the lives of our comrades-in-arms to the cause of its freedom, of its welfare, and of its exaltation among the nations.

The Irish Republic is entitled to, and hereby claims, the allegiance of every Irishman and Irishwoman. The Republic guarantees religious and civil liberty, equal rights and equal opportunities to all its citizens, and declares its resolve to pursue the happiness and prosperity of the whole nation and of all its parts, cherishing all the children of the nation equally, and oblivious of the differences carefully fostered by an alien government, which have divided a minority from the majority in the past.

Until our arms have brought the opportune moment for the establishment of a permanent National Government, representative of the whole people of Ireland, and elected by the suffrages of all her men and women, the Provisional Government, hereby constituted, will administer the civil and military affairs of the Republic in trust for the people.

We place the cause of the Irish Republic under the protection of the Most High God, Whose blessing we invoke upon our arms, and we pray that no one who serves that cause will dishonour it by cowardice, inhumanity or rapine. In this supreme hour the Irish nation must, by its valour and discipline and by the readiness of its children to sacrifice themselves for the common good, prove itself worthy of the august destiny to which it is called.

Signed on Behalf of the Provisional Government,

THOMAS J. CLARKE
SEAN MACDIARMADA   THOMAS MACDONAGH
P. H. PEARSE   EAMONN CEANNT
JAMES CONNOLLY   JOSEPH PLUNKETT

Pearse, Connolly, Clarke, Plunkett, and MacDiarmada all fought at the GPO. Ceannt lead the forces at the South Dublin Union and MacDonagh those at Jacob's Biscuit Factory.[2] All seven who signed the proclamation lived through Easter week but eventually paid for their audacity with their lives.

Having called the Irish Republic into existence, Pearse, its president and commander in chief, returned to the GPO, the home of the provisional government, and the flag of the republic was hoisted over the building, where it remained for six days.

POBLACHT NA H EIREANN.

THE PROVISIONAL GOVERNMENT
OF THE
IRISH REPUBLIC
TO THE PEOPLE OF IRELAND.

IRISHMEN AND IRISHWOMEN : In the name of God and of the dead generations from which she receives her old tradition of nationhood, Ireland, through us, summons her children to her flag and strikes for her freedom.

Having organised and trained her manhood through her secret revolutionary organisation, the Irish Republican Brotherhood, and through her open military organisations, the Irish Volunteers and the Irish Citizen Army, having patiently perfected her discipline, having resolutely waited for the right moment to reveal itself, she now seizes that moment, and, supported by her exiled children in America and by gallant allies in Europe, but relying in the first on her own strength, she strikes in full confidence of victory.

We declare the right of the people of Ireland to the ownership of Ireland, and to the unfettered control of Irish destinies, to be sovereign and indefeasible. The long usurpation of that right by a foreign people and government has not extinguished the right, nor can it ever be extinguished except by the destruction of the Irish people. In every generation the Irish people have asserted their right to national freedom and sovereignty : six times during the past three hundred years they have asserted it in arms. Standing on that fundamental right and again asserting it in arms in the face of the world, we hereby proclaim the Irish Republic as a Sovereign Independent State, and we pledge our lives and the lives of our comrades-in-arms to the cause of its freedom, of its welfare, and of its exaltation among the nations.

The Irish Republic is entitled to, and hereby claims, the allegiance of every Irishman and Irishwoman. The Republic guarantees religious and civil liberty, equal rights and equal opportunities to all its citizens, and declares its resolve to pursue the happiness and prosperity of the whole nation and of all its parts, cherishing all the children of the nation equally, and oblivious of the differences carefully fostered by an alien government, which have divided a minority from the majority in the past.

Until our arms have brought the opportune moment for the establishment of a permanent National Government, representative of the whole people of Ireland and elected by the suffrages of all her men and women, the Provisional Government, hereby constituted, will administer the civil and military affairs of the Republic in trust for the people.

We place the cause of the Irish Republic under the protection of the Most High God, Whose blessing we invoke upon our arms, and we pray that no one who serves that cause will dishonour it by cowardice, inhumanity, or rapine. In this supreme hour the Irish nation must, by its valour and discipline and by the readiness of its children to sacrifice themselves for the common good, prove itself worthy of the august destiny to which it is called.

Signed on Behalf of the Provisional Government,

THOMAS J. CLARKE.

SEAN Mac DIARMADA. THOMAS MacDONAGH.
P. H. PEARSE. EAMONN CEANNT.
JAMES CONNOLLY. JOSEPH PLUNKETT.

Proclamation of the Irish Republic.

Pearse and his colleagues did not expect to defeat the British army, for how could they? As James Connolly left Liberty Hall, he confessed to a friend, "We're going out to be slaughtered, you know."[3] But he went because he and other leaders believed that Ireland was slumbering and only a heroic gesture, a blood sacrifice, an act of voluntary martyrdom, could reawaken republican nationalism in Ireland. MacDiarmada wrote from his cell in Kilmainham Prison on the eve of his execution, "We die that the Irish nation may live. Our blood will rebaptise and reinvigorate the land."[4]

In the early months of the war, a sign on Liberty Hall had read, "We serve neither King nor Kaiser, but Ireland," and all the evidence now available indicates this to have been true. At the time, however, the British government, and perhaps a majority of the Irish, saw things very differently. The reference to "gallant allies in Europe," the Germans, in the Proclamation of the Irish Republic, had been a rhetorical flourish, but Lord Wimborne's proclamation on Easter Monday spoke very seriously of "an attempt, instigated and designated by the foreign enemies of our king and country."[5] The London *Times* of April 26, 1916 spoke of "a carefully-arranged plot, concocted between the Irish traitors and their German confederates." John Redmond, the leader of the Irish Party in Parliament since 1900, accused the rebels of insanely destroying forty years of progress towards Irish self-government. Of the Rising, he said on April 28, "Germany plotted it, Germany organized it, Germany paid for it."[6] The British government believed that zeppelin attacks on London and the shelling of English east coast ports by German warships had been coordinated with the Rising to divert military attention from the event in Ireland.

To the government, then, this was not simply an Irish rebellion against the United Kingdom, which would have been bad enough in the middle of a great war: it was a German plot which had to be crushed. The government moved quickly to bring in troop reinforcements, artillery, armored cars, and even a gunboat, which began to operate on the River Liffey at the end of Sackville Street, within sight of the GPO, on Wednesday. By 4:00 P.M. on Monday, reinforcements had begun to arrive in Dublin from barracks at the Curragh, County Kildare, fifty miles southwest of Dublin. By early Tuesday morning there were 4,650 soldiers from Ireland in Dublin, and more were to come. Martial law was proclaimed for Dublin that evening and for the whole of Ireland the following day, Wednesday. Reinforcements from England began to arrive in the city that day, which was also the day Sir John Maxwell was assigned to command the operation. By the end of the week, about 12,000 U.K. government troops were ranged against about 1,500 Irish republicans.

The government had acted decisively, but cautiously. Throughout the week it lacked information concerning the strength of the republicans, and for a short while it feared both a general uprising in the country and a German invasion. The military plan adopted in Dublin was to overwhelm the republicans with artillery and superior numbers over a period of days, not to storm republican positions. Beginning on Tuesday, the army isolated republican strongholds from each other. It occupied a line just south of the River Liffey, from Kingsbridge Station in the west to Trinity College in the east. It also cordoned off the inner city north of the river, and placed two smaller cordons around the Four Courts and the GPO.

With the exception of the battle for Mount Street Bridge and a sixteen-hour battle at North King Street, there were no major engagements between the two forces. The republicans were well entrenched and attempts to storm their positions would have meant heavy government casualties, as happened unnecessarily at Mount Street Bridge on Wednesday afternoon when the army could have retreated and used other routes into the city. The GPO was shelled by artillery, machine-gun and rifle fire for five days from a considerable distance, but no attempt was made at an assault. Indeed, republicans occupied the major buildings for about one hundred yards around the GPO virtually until the surrender, finally yielding not to an attack but to a raging fire. Incendiary shells from government artillery set fire to buildings in Abbey Street on Thursday morning. The fire spread to Sackville Street, and at 4:00 P.M. on Friday the GPO itself was hit and caught fire. By 7:00 P.M. the building had to be evacuated. Five leaders of the Rising, Pearse, Clarke, Plunkett, MacDermott, and Connolly, the latter crippled by a bullet wound he received in the street on Thursday, spent their last night of freedom in a small house on Moore Street, just behind the GPO.

By Friday evening, the republicans had taken considerable casualties from four days of almost continuous artillery and rifle fire, and Sackville Street and its surroundings had been devastated, but there had been no decisive battle. Some of the republican positions, Jacob's Biscuit Factory and Boland's Mill, for example, had seen relatively little action. Nevertheless, on Saturday Pearse and Connolly decided to surrender. They had been forced out of the burning GPO and were surrounded. An attempt to link up with their colleagues in the Four Courts was impossible because of the British cordon. Their shell-shocked troops had been contained for four days in the GPO, casualties had been heavy, and supplies were short. Furthermore, Dublin had suffered terribly. Parts of the city were devastated by artillery and fire. Hundreds had been trapped in their homes by the crossfire of snipers hidden in buildings and behind street barricades, and many innocent people had been killed by stray bullets. The republicans had made their point, and the GPO headquarters group were ready to surrender. Pearse knew that death awaited him no matter what the immediate outcome of the Rising, and on Friday morning, knowing the end was near, he prepared a statement for his troops which said, "I am satisfied that we have saved Ireland's honour."[7]

At 12:45 P.M. on Saturday, April 29, a republican nurse, Elizabeth O'Farrell, who had been in the GPO from the beginning, left Moore Street under the protection of a white flag to announce that Pearse was ready to discuss a surrender. She was told that the surrender had to be unconditional. At 2:30 P.M. Pearse himself accompanied O'Farrell. He was taken to General Maxwell and signed his general surrender order at 3:45 P.M. It was later cosigned by James Connolly and Thomas MacDonagh. Nurse O'Farrell and a British officer carried the order to each of the republican positions around the city, finishing on Sunday. Only the GPO had been lost of all the major sites occupied in strength on Monday. Hundreds of republicans had survived at the Four Courts, the South Dublin Union, Jacob's Biscuit Factory, the College of Surgeons, and Boland's Mill, and many of them felt that the Rising should continue, but the surrender order was accepted. The remnants of the republican army were taken into custody and marched through a shocked and relieved city on Sunday morning.

The Rising, in its most immediate sense, was over, although random firing could still be heard the following Tuesday. Precise casualty figures are difficult to obtain, but in the official reckoning about 450 died, and 2,500 hundred were wounded.[8] The republican and civilian dead were difficult to distinguish from each other, but it was estimated that over sixty rebels had died.

The republicans were certainly not received as heroes as they surrendered. The country had not risen in their support, and the Irish Party in Parliament had condemned them. Outside Dublin, support for the Rising had been minuscule. Republicans had captured some positions in County Galway, County Wexford, and County Louth, but no major city or town had staged its own rising.

The population of Dublin, where normal life had ceased on Easter Monday, had been more than simply inconvenienced. Many had paid with their lives. In the cordoned inner city, food supplies had run out and were seriously disrupted elsewhere in the city. Gas supplies for cooking and light had been cut for most of the city on Monday. Soon banks and many work places and shops were closed, and public transport and postal services ceased. The inner city housed some of the worst slums in Europe, and the slum poor looted much of Sackville Street in the first days of the Rising. At another point on the social scale, the middle class regarded the Rising with horror. Redmond Fitzgerald described these feelings:

> The insurrection had not carried the people with it. The crowds who poured out of the tenements did not feel at one with these grim young men who gave them orders and pushed them back from the shops that lay bursting with things they had coveted all their pinched lives. It did not carry the lace-curtain Irish with it either, for respectable lives were being disrupted and you dare not go the grocers. So the two Dublins, who hated each other, united in contempt for these upstarts and their Republic.[9]

The Easter Rising was not a popular rebellion, not on Sunday, April 30, when Dubliners inspected a scene in central Dublin reminiscent of newspaper photographs of war-shattered towns in France and Belgium. But though few yet realized it, the Rising had accomplished a great deal. One who recognized this very quickly was the writer James Stephens, who had already completed an eyewitness account for publication by May 6. He wrote, "[Ireland] was not with the revolution, but in a few months she will be, and her heart which was withering will be warmed by the knowledge that men have thought her worth dying for."[10] Another who quickly came to understand was W. B. Yeats, who was in England during the Rising but described his feelings in the poem, *Easter 1916*, composed in September of that year. He had not liked or been impressed by the leaders of the Rising as he knew them in the past. He was polite to them, the poets Pearse and MacDonagh, for example, but condescending. Of Countess Constance Markiewicz, he wrote in the poem:

> That woman's days were spent
> In ignorant good-will
> Her nights in arguments
> Until her voice grew shrill.

He thought John MacBride, who was executed on May 5, "A drunken, vainglorious lout." But, Yeats confessed:

> He, too, has been changed in his turn,
> Transformed utterly:

In his final stanza, Yeats paid tribute to the Rising:

> And what if excess of love
> Bewildered them till they died?
> I write it out in verse—
> MacDonagh and MacBride
> And Connolly and Pearse
> Now and in time to be,
> Wherever green is worn,
> Are changed, changed utterly:
> A terrible beauty is born.[11]

1 Redmond Fitzgerald, *Cry Blood, Cry Erin* (New York, 1966), p. 75.

2 Sean MacDiarmada's name in English was John MacDermott. Ceannt was known as Edward Kent.

3 Fitzgerald, p. 79.

4 Ibid., p. 109.

5 Charles Duff, *Six Days to Shake an Empire* (New York, 1966), p. 121.

6 London *Times*, 29 April 1916.

7 Max Caulfield, *The Easter Rebellion* (London, 1965), p. 309.

8 Great Britain, *Documents Relative to the Sinn Fein Movement*, Cmd. 1108, xxix, 429, 1921, pp. 14–15.

9 Fitzgerald, p. 88.

10 James Stephens, *The Insurrection in Dublin* (Dublin, 1966) p. 8.

11 W. B. Yeats, *Collected Poems* (London, 1958), pp. 202–205.

CHAPTER 2

England and Ireland
Before the Union of 1801

WHAT WAS IT THAT LED A FEW REPUBLICANS TO REBEL
at a time when most Irish men and women believed that the United
Kingdom was fighting a just war in Europe? The reasons are complex,
and to understand them we have to start at the beginning of the stormy
political relationship between the islands of Ireland and Britain in the
twelfth century. The Easter Rising was not inevitable, but it was the
understandable consequence of past encounters.

THE CONQUEST OF IRELAND

In approximately 1155, the English-born Pope Adrian IV granted
the lordship of Ireland to King Henry II of England in his *Laudabiliter*,
a papal bull or edict.[1] Irish nationalists subsequently charged that the
only English pope in the history of the Catholic Church authorized
the English conquest of Ireland. This misrepresents what happened in
several ways. First, Adrian was not an English imperialist. His inten-
tion, it appears, was to bring the Irish church firmly under the "jurisdiction of St. Peter and of the holy Roman Church," in the language of
the bull. Second, Henry II was Norman French, not English. The
Normans had invaded England in 1066, and the English nation as we
know it today had not been defined in 1155.

When the Normans actually went to Ireland, in 1169, it was primarily as adventurers, not imperialists. Furthermore, it was at the invi-
tation of an Irish king, Dermot MacMurrough, who recruited a number of Normans and Welsh to assist him to recover the throne of

Leinster, one of many kingdoms in Ireland. A much larger force, under the earl of Pembroke, known as Strongbow, landed in 1170. Strongbow married the daughter of Dermot and secured the throne of Leinster for himself on the death of the king. It was to check the growth of what Henry II feared might be a rival Norman state in Ireland, under Strongbow, that Henry landed in Ireland in 1171. He confirmed Strongbow's claim to Leinster in return for a pledge of loyalty to the Crown and received the homage of other kings in Ireland. Henry held court in Dublin for some months, but his presence fell far short of conquest. The Normans did not conquer Ireland as they had conquered England, and they never conducted a census, an Irish equivalent of the Domesday Book which formed the basis of the Norman state in England in 1086. Henry held the lordship of Ireland essentially in name only because the country continued to be governed by kings and chiefs who were either native Irish or, following Strongbow, Normans. For centuries Ireland remained what it had been before the Normans came, an arena for local rivalries and wars. It was not governed from England in any real sense and was too torn by internal warfare to govern itself as a single state.

The kings of England sought to manage Ireland through a feudal pact between the Crown and Irish kings and chiefs. The system failed because the Crown could not physically control the rivalries and ambitions of the local rulers, many of whom were native Irish with no appreciation of feudal allegiance. The Norman settlers were themselves too far from the throne to be easily managed, and many were transformed into a new class by intermarriage with the native Irish. The Statutes of Kilkenny, 1366, were designed to prevent the dilution of Norman stock by intermarriage. In the eastern and central parts of Ireland, settlers were forbidden to adopt the Irish language and culture, and the native Irish were required to adopt English ways. The rest of the country was abandoned to the native Irish.

The Norman policy failed but it did contribute to the sense that there were two Irelands, a settlers' Ireland and a native, or Gaelic, Ireland. The Crown possessed only nominal control of the settled portion of the country, where the Statutes of Kilkenny were not rigidly enforced, but into this area law, government, and feudal forms of social organization were imported from England. For example, an Irish

Exchequer was created in 1200, and an Irish Parliament on the English model was established in Dublin before the end of the thirteenth century. Gaelic Ireland never developed native legal and political institutions which might have formed the foundations of a united Ireland and instead, as the historian J. C. Beckett writes, "The very notion of an Irish state with an effective central government is part of Ireland's English heritage."[2]

The Irish Parliament was never strong. It sat very infrequently, only three times during the forty-five-year reign of Elizabeth I, for example, and its power was limited by two laws. The first was Poyning's Law of 1495, passed by the Irish Parliament itself. This specified that all Irish bills had to be presented to the King and Council in England for approval before they could be considered in the Irish Parliament. By the late seventeenth century, the Irish Parliament was initiating bills itself, but they still required the English government's formal approval, through the monarch, before passage in Ireland, and this relationship continued until 1782. Second, in the Declaratory Act of 1720 the British Parliament asserted its right to legislate for Ireland. Despite these interventions from England, the notion that Ireland was a separate political community was nourished by the Irish Parliament, and the bulk of settlers who adhered to English cultural, social, political, and legal forms, saw themselves as a distinct class, not English exactly, but the English of Ireland.

It was two Tudor monarchs, Henry VIII (1509–47) and Elizabeth I (1558–1603), who finally brought about the English conquest of Ireland, although even they could not extinguish the sense that Ireland was a separate political community. Furthermore, by the sixteenth century the Reformation had added a religious dimension to Anglo-Irish relations because the great majority of the Irish, whether of native or settler stock, remained Roman Catholic. As a result, during the later Tudor period, Ireland became an important target for Roman Catholic Spain. Henry II had feared a rival Norman state in Ireland but the Protestant Tudors, Henry VIII and Elizabeth, feared a rival Spanish Ireland. The papal bull *Laudabiliter* of 1154 assigned Ireland to Henry II of England, but the bull *Rex Hiberniae* of 1555 assigned it to Philip II of Spain and his wife, Queen Mary I, the Roman Catholic queen of England from 1553–58.[3]

By the early sixteenth century, the zone of even nominal royal control in Ireland had been reduced to a fifty-by-twenty mile area around Dublin, the so-called Pale. Even there the earls of Kildare had ruled virtually independently as the kings' deputies for several generations. The greater part of the country was still controlled by the native Irish or the Old English, descendants of the Norman settlers. Ireland was a land of political instability, poor roads, negligible urban development in the interior, and primitive agriculture, with very little contact with the broader cultural life of Europe. It was regarded in England as a wild and savage place on the edge of the world; as virgin territory, like Virginia, it was ripe for settlement by agents of London companies.

Henry VIII moved to change at least the political facts of Ireland. In 1534, the earl of Kildare was exiled to England, where he died in prison, and his five sons were subsequently executed for rebellion. The power of the Kildares was therefore broken in the Pale which came firmly under the control of the Crown. In 1536 and 1537, the Irish Parliament recognized the supremacy of Henry VIII over the church in Ireland, but whilst the Irish bishops accepted this at first, they were soon alienated by Henry's dissolution of monasteries, and as a result the Reformation never came to Ireland. Resistance to English authority, by both the native Irish and the Old English, came to be linked inextricably to the Roman Catholic Church, whose authority in Ireland was never extinguished.

Having broken the Kildares in the Pale, Henry sought to strengthen his hold on the rest of the country by using a policy of surrender and regrant. All the chiefs and kings of Ireland were required to surrender their lands to the Crown which then regranted them under the feudal relationship to the king of knight service. The Irish were also required to abandon Irish names and customs and were entitled to maintain armed forces only with the consent of the Crown. Their land would be forfeited if they rebelled. Henry's policy confirmed the titles of the Old English, who already held their land in a feudal relationship to the crown, but it represented an attack on the traditional native Irish land tenure system in which land was the property of an extended family group, not the chief and his immediate heirs. Finally, in 1541, the Irish Parliament recognized Henry VIII as King of Ireland rather than lord, the title that had been used since the time of Henry II.

Tudor policies, which included the assertion of the king's supremacy over the Irish church, the surrender and regrant of lands, and the new title, King of Ireland, did not actually pacify the country nor did they significantly extend the Crown's authority beyond the Pale, but they had the negative effect of alienating the Roman Catholics of Ireland from England. For the remainder of the Tudor period, England feared an alliance between Catholic Spain and the Catholic Irish because England still lacked physical control of the island. It was left to Elizabeth I (1558–1603) to bring about the final conquest of Ireland by applying the force which had always been absent before.

Elizabeth took the throne of England in 1558 and quickly asserted the formal authority of the Crown over both church and state in Ireland with the Acts of Uniformity and Supremacy, 1560; she did not make the mistake of rigidly enforcing the new laws. There were areas which remained almost purely Gaelic, as well as Catholic, in Ireland, notably Ulster in the north, in which the Irish, or Brehon, legal system prevailed. The central administration in Dublin was placed in the hands of new Protestant settlers from England, but the Catholic Old English dominated commerce and the law, and when Ireland was divided into counties, Catholics predominated in local administration. Refusing to swear an oath accepting the religious supremacy of the Crown was not an absolute barrier to political or judicial office in Ireland because Elizabeth was more concerned with the loyalty of her subjects than their religion. This prudent policy meant that she retained the loyalty of a great many Irish during her reign, despite three major Irish rebellions and military intervention from Spain. In 1601, four thousand Spanish troops landed in Kinsale, south of Cork, in an unsuccessful invasion.

Irish rebellions were symptomatic of the fact that Elizabeth was engaged in almost continuous efforts to subdue Ireland during her reign, and it was not until she sent Lord Mountjoy as the queen's lord deputy in 1600 that England (no longer Norman but now indisputably English) was able to complete the conquest that the Normans had begun more than four hundred years before. Mountjoy broke the Ulster rebellions of Hugh O'Neill, earl of Tyrone, and Hugh Roe O'Donnell, earl of Tyreconnell, and the war was won just days after Elizabeth's death in 1603.

The conquest was complete, but the seeds had been sown for discord to come. The failure of the Reformation in Ireland and the resilience of the Old English and native Irish, both of them Roman Catholic, meant that while England could now enforce its military and political authority in Ireland, it could not enforce its spiritual or moral authority. Very little effort was made to convert the Irish either from Roman Catholicism or from the Gaelic culture. Acts of Parliament had been passed to suppress both, but conversion was not practiced. Catholicism survived, and despite the gradual spread of the English language and customs, the Gaelic culture persisted among the native Irish, who were the majority of the population. The two identities, Roman Catholic and native Irish, or Gaelic, always separated the majority in Ireland from the Anglo-Protestant minority.

THE PLANTATIONS AND CROMWELL'S CONFISCATIONS

The Protestant population of Ireland was extremely small until "plantation" began in the seventeenth century in Ireland. This was the policy of settlement of "loyal" English or Scottish immigrants. Queen Mary attempted plantations on a relatively small scale in the mid-sixteenth century, as did Elizabeth, her successor, but large-scale settlement only began during the reign of Elizabeth's Stuart successor, James I (1603–25), from 1610 onwards. It was assisted by the "flight of the earls" in 1607, when the great earls of Tyrone and Tyreconnell and approximately one hundred chiefs left Ulster, the most Gaelic of the Irish provinces, with their supporters. Their lands in six of the nine Ulster counties were declared forfeit and assigned to agents to lease to English or Scottish settlers. Derry City, for example, was awarded to the City of London in 1610 and was renamed Londonderry.

In this way, a new class of settlers, largely Scottish and Presbyterian, came to Ulster. Unlike their Norman predecessors, they tended not to intermarry or adopt Irish customs, and they remained apart from the Roman Catholic Irish. Those Catholics who managed to acquire or retain farms in Ulster settled the poorest land, and there began the economic, social, and religious segregation that has characterized the northeastern counties of Ireland ever since. There also began that sense of outrage, of colonial exploitation and oppression, that still influences Catholics in Northern Ireland. They are the dispossessed. The contemporary conflict between Protestants and Catholics in Northern Ireland has origins, therefore, in the seventeenth-century settlement of Ulster.

The success of the Ulster plantation led to other, smaller plantations, farther south, in Wexford, Longford, Leitrim, and Connaught. By 1641 approximately 40 percent of Ireland was owned by Protestants, and approximately 200,000 English and 130,000 Scottish Presbyterian settlers had made their homes in Ireland. They were not solely in the north, but the scale of the Ulster plantation was unparalleled, as was its effect on relations between the Catholic and Protestant communities.

Under James I there was a more determined attempt than hitherto to ensure that the central administration of Ireland was Protestant, but the Tudor laws against Catholicism were still not strictly enforced for fear of provoking new and costly rebellions. It was only with considerable difficulty, and by creating new parliamentary boroughs, that the Irish administration was able to secure a Protestant majority in the Irish Parliament, and there were times when the Catholic and Protestant elites made common cause against the Crown's demands for subsidies. Indeed, it was a combination of Protestants and Catholics in Parliament that led to the impeachment and subsequent execution of the king's Irish deputy, the earl of Strafford, in 1641.

In return for their willingness to support subsidies to the king, Catholics in Ireland, particularly the Old English, suffered less in the practice of their politics, occupations, and religion than might have been expected, but they were not conciliated. In 1641, during the English civil war, a bloody uprising occurred among the remaining native Catholic gentry of Ulster which spread to much of Ireland. In the growing disorder the Catholic Old English combined forces with their coreligionists, the native Irish, in a Catholic confederacy. Owen Roe O'Neill, an exiled Catholic, came from service in the Spanish army in 1642 to lead the rebel army, with a military organization centered on the town of Kilkenny, seventy miles south of Dublin. However, following the victory of the Puritans in England, Oliver Cromwell was appointed lord lieutenant of Ireland in 1649 and he launched vicious reprisals, including infamous massacres of Catholics at Drogheda and

Wexford. Furthermore, in the Act of Settlement of 1652, the Catholic estates of Ireland, with the exception of those in Connaught, the most desolate part of the country, and surrounding areas, were confiscated and distributed among those who had fought in or financed Cromwell's campaign. Six thousand Catholics lost their lands, forty thousand fled into exile, and one hundred thousand were transported to the Americas. Some land was returned to Catholics when Charles II was restored to the throne in 1660, but 80 percent of Ireland remained in Protestant hands. The Tudor conquest, the Stuart Plantations, and the Cromwellian confiscations had effected an enormous transfer of land, wealth, and political power from Catholics to Protestants in Ireland.

The conquest and plantations provided the bases for a united Ireland for the first time. As Jim Mac Laughlin writes, "It took plantation and English rule to turn the fragmented world of Gaelic Ireland into a far more unified political space."[4] But Irish Catholicism remained as a barrier to full political integration. The Catholics would not deny their religion nor could they all be driven out. Indeed, they were needed as tenants and laborers in areas now owned by Protestants, many of whom were absentee owners, a class that was to plague Ireland for another 250 years. As historian Patrick O'Farrell notes, "[T]he Irish occupants lived in a land they no longer owned, and the English owners, by and large, owned a land in which they did not live."[5] Some members of the Catholic upper class held onto, or subsequently recovered, their lands, and Catholics managed to prosper in trade, an activity not closed to them by law, but they no longer owned the bulk of the land, and Cromwell destroyed their political role. These facts were confirmed by the events of 1688 to 1691.

In 1685 the Catholic James II became king, but the Catholics' hopes for emancipation were dashed by his removal from the throne in the English revolution of 1688 and his replacement by the Protestant couple, William of Orange and Queen Mary II, the daughter of James. With the support of Louis XIV of France, James went to Ireland in 1689 to launch a campaign for his restoration. He summoned a parliament in Dublin and formed an army but was defeated by William of Orange at the battle of the Boyne in 1690. In Northern Ireland this is celebrated every July in triumphalist parades as a great Irish Protestant victory, as is the famous Protestant resistence to King James at the

siege of Derry. At the time, however, the war had much broader implications than a conflict of religions in Ireland. James had the support
of Louis XIV of France, who was using Ireland as a means to distract
William from European concerns. A mixture of Catholic and Protestant Irish, French, German, and Walloon (or French-speaking Belgian)
troops fought for James, while a mixture of Irish, Dutch, German, and
Danish troops fought in William's army. Nonetheless, the end of the
war, which came with the Treaty of Limerick in 1691, had dire consequences for Irish Catholics. It led to the expropriation of still more
Catholic land so that, by the turn of the century, Catholic holdings in
Ireland had been reduced to about 15 percent of the total.

THE PENAL LAWS AND THE ANGLO-IRISH ASCENDANCY

To protect the lands and political power they had won in the seventeenth century, the Protestant-controlled Irish Parliament began to
approve a series of penal laws in 1695. These expelled the Catholic
bishops from the country and required priests to register and renounce
the Pope. The laws denied Catholics the right to vote or sit in parliament, practice law, buy land, maintain schools, send their children
abroad to be educated, or own horses worth more than £5 each. The
common-law principle of primogeniture which protected large estates
(the oldest son inherits, keeping his father's estate intact) was denied
to Catholics. Any remaining Catholic estates had to be equally divided
among all the sons on the death of an owner unless there was a Protestant son to inherit the whole.

The penal laws were directed primarily against Catholics, but some,
by preferring the Anglican Church of Ireland, worked against the substantial Presbyterian community in Ulster too. There were also a number of British policies which discriminated against the Irish as a whole,
both Catholic and Protestant.[6] In the Declaratory Act of 1720, for example, the British Parliament in London asserted a right to legislate
directly for Ireland, which is to say, to bypass the Irish Parliament at its
discretion.

When simply listed in this way, the penal laws are horrifying, but
fortunately they were not strictly enforced. Indeed, they could not have
been enforced without transforming Ireland into a totalitarian soci-

ety, which never happened. Many of the Catholic clergy evaded registration and bishops continued to be appointed to Ireland. Catholic children often went abroad to study, and Catholic schools even existed in Ireland in the eighteenth century. Catholics also found ways to evade the laws concerning landownership—the use of Protestant nominees to own land, for example, or even nominal conversions of owners. Neither the Catholic Church nor middle-class Catholic commercial interests, nor even Catholic landowners and a small surviving Catholic aristocracy, were completely suppressed. When the penal laws were lifted late in the eighteenth century there was a substantial Catholic professional and commercial class which the laws, by inhibiting alternative activities, had inadvertently strengthened. Kevin Whelan, the Irish historian, called this class "an underground gentry."[7] There were, for example, Catholic "middlemen" who rented land which they subdivided to tenant farmers. They often controlled substantial holdings without being landowners. The Catholic Irish at the dawn of the nineteenth century were not, therefore, a wholly downtrodden people, but the penal laws succeeded in their primary purposes, which were to protect the Anglican Church of Ireland, deny Irish Catholics a legitimate role in Irish public life, and restrict Irish landownership. By 1776, Catholics, 75 percent of the population, owned only about 5 percent of the land of Ireland, and the great majority of Catholic farmers were tenants.

The eighteenth century proved to be a century of unflattering contrasts in Ireland, because as the Protestants introduced the discriminatory penal laws, they simultaneously entered a period of extraordinary accomplishment. This was the age of the Anglo-Irish Ascendancy, when an Anglican upper class formed a sophisticated political, legal, and social elite. They were substantially more than an aristocracy because they included many who had made their own way in life, in the professions, for example. The Ascendancy class included the great Anglo-Irish writers, Swift, Berkeley, Goldsmith, Sheridan and Burke, for example, who flourished in the east of Ireland even as a Gaelic literature survived in the south and west. It was a century of great country houses, and Dublin became a very great city, as one can still see today in what is left of Georgian Dublin architecture. It was also a century of intense political activity by Ascendancy Protestants who inherited the belief that Ireland was a distinct political community. They spoke of themselves as "the Irish nation," and while this notion excluded the majority of the Catholic population, the Protestant Irish, or Anglo-Irish, knew that Ireland was distinct from England, as they were distinct from the English.[8]

Until the 1760s, British administration in Ireland was largely indirect, through the king's deputy or lord lieutenant. In the eighteenth century the lord lieutenant rarely visited the country and leading members of the Ascendancy acted as agents for the Crown, but their power was diminished from the 1760s when senior British officials became resident in Dublin. Furthermore, the independence of the exclusively Protestant Irish Parliament was undermined, because many members were the nominees of English absentee landowners or received positions and pensions from the Crown in return for their support. As the historian W. E. H. Lecky wrote, "The lavish distribution of peerages had proved to be the cheapest and most efficacious means of governing Ireland."[9] Nevertheless, the eighteenth century increasingly saw Irish politicians, all of them Protestants, oppose a range of British policies for Ireland, particularly taxes, finance, and imperial trade policy and agitate for political equality with Britain. What they wanted was a genuinely independent Irish Parliament, one free of British manipulation, under a shared Crown. Indeed, for a short period at the end of the century they achieved this status because their agitation for political freedom coincided with a similar movement in the American colonies, the American War of Independence from 1776 to 1781.

In the eighteenth century Irish Protestants established volunteer militia groups numbering about forty thousand, ostensibly to defend the country against France, but when the number of British soldiers stationed in Ireland was depleted by the American war, it became clear that the volunteers were in a position to overwhelm the British garrison, and the government found it prudent to yield to parliamentary leaders' demands for greater independence. In 1779, free trade in Irish goods was permitted, and in 1782 Britain agreed to the demand articulated by Henry Grattan and Henry Flood that there should be an independent Irish parliament. The Irish Parliament itself repealed Poyning's Law of 1494, without repercussions from Britain, and the British Parliament repealed the Declaratory Act of 1720. This resulted in the so-called "Irish Constitution of 1782," which meant that after

1782 there was no requirement that Irish bills be submitted to the King in Council in Britain for approval before their introduction in Ireland, and the Irish Parliament was the only one that could legislate for Ireland.

These years of parliamentary independence did not prove to be golden for Ireland. There were, it is true, significant improvements for Catholics. For example, most of the penal laws were abolished between 1778 and 1792, and Catholics were allowed to vote from 1793, subject to a property qualification. In addition, a Catholic seminary was established at Maynooth, in County Kildare. But in 1795 the Irish Parliament rejected the Grattan bill that would have allowed Catholics to sit as members. Protestant members were willing to accept Grattan's leadership on Irish parliamentary independence but not on Irish parliamentary reform. One result was that the Irish Parliament continued to be influenced by Crown patronage, by absentee landlords, and by an Irish administration led by a lord lieutenant who was an agent of the Crown, appointed on the advice of the British government.

What should have been constitutionally clear after 1782, that Britain and Ireland were coequal states under one Crown, with separate parliaments, was murky because of the very different roles of the British and Irish governments. By the 1780s the British prime minister and cabinet had largely taken over the government of Britain from the monarch and one of the things they controlled, through their "advice" to the king, was his appointments to the Irish government in Dublin. Ireland could not really be independent unless it had its own prime minister and cabinet who were as free of British government control as the Irish Parliament was now free of the British Parliament. But this was not to be. So long as Britain controlled Crown appointments to the Irish administration, and so long as the Irish Parliament remained unreformed, Britain could manipulate the Irish political class through the royal patronage that the lord lieutenant controlled and the parliamentary members who were nominees of absentee landlords.

THE UNION

In the late 1790s, William Pitt, the British prime minister, concluded that the peace of Ireland and the economic health and security of Britain required the abolition of the Irish Parliament. Ireland had shown itself vulnerable to threats posed by violent secret societies, including the Society of the United Irishmen, which organized a rebellion with French support in 1798, and the Irish Parliament refused any overtures from Britain to negotiate an Anglo-Irish relationship which would have allowed imperial commercial and military policies to be set by Britain. The British government was also embarrassed by the "regency crisis" of 1788–89, during the mental illness of King George III. Both parliaments agreed that the heir to the throne, the Prince Regent, should act for the king, but whereas the British Parliament endorsed a regency with limited powers for the Prince of Wales, the Irish Parliament favored a regency with unconditional powers. The king recovered, and the crisis ended, but it had exposed to Britain the shortcomings of a shared monarchy.

There were reasons, then, for Britain to want to control Ireland which went well beyond the British political élite's concern for its property in Ireland and desire to protect the Anglican Church of Ireland, both of which were substantial interests. In short, if Britain wanted to direct an imperial trading system, be sure that a foreign enemy would not control its near neighbor, and protect the Crown, the Anglican Church, and property, it had to control Ireland as it had never done before. The solution was to abolish the Irish Parliament and create an integrated United Kingdom of Britain and Ireland.

By using Crown patronage, although bribery might be a better word, and the votes of the nominees of absentee landlords, the Irish Parliament was persuaded to vote for what the British government wanted, the Act of Union of 1800. The final vote in the Irish House of Commons was 58 to 115, but it took two attempts to secure this majority. The act abolished the Irish Parliament and bound Ireland and Britain together in a constitutional union of the United Kingdom. From January 1801 the two communities, Ireland and Britain, were merged for the first time ever in a single parliament, more than 800 years after the Normans first came to Ireland. Henceforward, Irish representatives would sit in the House of Commons in London, and representatives of the Irish peerage would sit in the House of Lords.

A great many Ascendancy Protestants opposed the union because they feared it would lead to Catholic emancipation, but they soon discovered that as a minority of no more than 25 percent in a largely

Catholic country, their interests could be better protected by the parliament of a largely Protestant United Kingdom than in Dublin. They subsequently came to interpret the union as a fundamental constitutional pact between themselves and Britain by which the latter would defend the economic, social, religious, and political supremacy of the Ascendancy Irish. When advocating Catholic emancipation in the Irish Parliament in 1795, Henry Grattan asked his fellow countrymen, "Are we to be a Protestant settlement or an Irish nation?"[10] Before the union, Irish Protestants saw themselves as the Irish nation. After the Union, they could more properly be described as a Protestant settlement, and the Irish nation came to mean almost exclusively the Catholic Irish.

CONCLUSION

We all have images of the past which are part fact and part imagination. An imperialist is apt to see his empire as a blessing to those he absorbs, but his victims are apt see the experience in a different light, idealizing the pre-imperial past or focusing upon their suffering under the yoke of the oppressor.

It is certainly understandable that an Irish nationalist would want to interpret Anglo-Irish relations as a tale of over seven hundred years of conquest, savage exploitation, and repression. The conquest can, indeed, be said to have begun in 1169 or 1170. There were numerous attempts to populate Ireland with "loyalists" from England and to dispossess the indigenous Irish, including the Norman and Tudor settlements and the great plantations of the Stuarts. There were bloody campaigns in Ireland by the forces of Elizabeth, Cromwell, and William of Orange. There were calculated attempts to drive out the Gaelic culture and suppress the Roman Catholic religion, including the Statutes of Kilkenny, the policy of surrender and regrant, the Acts of Supremacy and Uniformity, the Cromwellian Act of Settlement, and the Penal Laws. Finally, English mercantilism treated Ireland as an economic colony to be exploited for England's gain.

Without denying these events we nevertheless ought to qualify them. For example, the Irish were fighting each other long before the Normans arrived, and the fighting continued until the completion of the conquest in 1603. Irish history, therefore, was not necessarily more bloody because of the intervention of England. Furthermore, instead of holding Ireland by the sword since 1169, the so-called English conquest was, for more than four hundred years, not a conquest at all. Even after the Tudor conquest, English attempts to suppress the Gaelic culture and the Catholic religion were unsuccessful because they were not strictly enforced. England preferred a quiet Ireland to a converted one and, in the end, Catholicism survived in Ireland but suffered near-extinction in England, where the authority of the Crown could be exercised directly. As Roy Foster puts it for Ireland, "Catholics continued to occupy a curiously edgy position of formal inferiority combined with tacit toleration."[11] The Gaelic culture suffered much more than Irish Catholicism, but probably less because of repressive statutes than because of the political and social dominance of the settlers. The language of law and administration became English, and the sheer weight of English culture overwhelmed the Irish.

These qualifications may modify our image of English oppression to some degree, but it was imperialism and oppression nonetheless. Ireland was, after all, England's oldest colony. Furthermore, because of the successful attempts of Irish nationalists to raise national consciousness in the nineteenth century, the events of the past were remarkably fresh in the minds of the men and women who staged the Easter Rising in 1916. They saw English rule in the least favorable light and believed that nothing less than Irish independence would compensate for the enormity of England's crime against Ireland.

1 Edmund Curtis and R. B. McDowell, eds., *Irish Historical Documents, 1172–1922* (New York, 1968), p. 17.

2 J. C. Beckett, *The Anglo-Irish Tradition* (London, 1976), p. 22.

3 Patrick O'Farrell, *Ireland's English Question: Anglo-Irish Relations, 1534–1970* (London, 1971), p. 20.

4 Jim Mac Laughlin, *Reimagining the Nation-State* (London, 2001), p. 62.

5 O'Farrell, p. 38.

6 After the Act of Union between England and Scotland in 1707 it was better to use the words Britain and British than England and English, although Irish nationalists always considered England the real enemy.

7 Cited by Mac Laughlin, p. 151.

8 Beckett, pp. 44–83.

9 W. E. H. Lecky, *A History of Ireland in the Eighteenth Century,* abridged by L. P. Curtis, Jr., (Chicago, 1972), p. 201.

10 O'Farrell, p. 63.

11 Roy Foster, *Modern Ireland, 1600–1972* (London, 1988), p. 121.

CHAPTER 3

Ireland and Irish Nationalism After the Union

THE SECOND HALF OF THE NINETEENTH CENTURY SAW the beginning of a conflict between a Catholic Irish nationalism and a Protestant counter nationalism, or unionism, that was to lead to the Easter Rising in 1916 and the partition of Ireland in 1921. Following chapters will consider various aspects of these two movements, but this chapter considers two important nineteenth-century developments that provide context for the discussion. The first was a set of radical changes in Irish society. The second was the emergence of nationalist ideologies and nationalist movements in Europe.

CHANGES IN IRELAND IN THE NINETEENTH CENTURY

When we speak of Irish nationalism we invariably mean the nationalism of the Catholic community, so it is important to note that Irish Catholicism in 1900 was very different from Irish Catholicism at the time of the union. The Irish Catholic Church was not a strong institution in 1801, nor were the Catholic Irish a particularly devout people. A change was led by Paul Cullen, who was appointed primate of Ireland and archbishop of Armagh in 1849, and subsequently archbishop of Dublin in 1852. Under his leadership, the Irish Catholic Church became the extraordinarily powerful institution it is today, and the Irish came to be one of the most devout Catholic communities in the world. Even as the Catholic population of Ireland was declining dramatically in the second half of the century, the number of priests and nuns was rising equally dramatically, as was the number of churches. This "devotional revolution," as Emmet Larkin describes it, was extremely important for Irish nationalism because of an alliance that was forged between nationalism and the church in the 1880s.[1]

Irish society as a whole was also very different in 1900 from what it had been at the time of the union. Until the great famine of 1845 to 1848, there was a huge peasant class in Ireland living on very small, rented plots of land with a diet based largely on the potato. Ireland's population doubled to over 8 million in the half century before the famine as the introduction of potato culture made possible the division of farms into smaller units, some less than five acres, enabling Irish sons and daughters to marry and raise children at a younger age. The condition of the Irish economy improved in these years but the plight of those on its margins was miserable and uncertain. The precarious situation owed something to a system of absentee landlords, most of them Protestants, whose properties were progressively subdivided into very small holdings by layers of middlemen. But the greater part of the blame must be laid on overpopulation and the subsequent pressure on agricultural land to produce sufficient food. As Roy Foster notes, "[We] are presented with a picture of population growth within an economy structurally unable, in the long run, to cope with it."[2]

Such was the situation on the land when the potato famine came in 1845. Famines were frequent in Ireland but the "great famine" was of epic proportions, in part because it lasted so long—until 1848—and was accompanied by additional agricultural distress, such as a bad grain harvest in 1848. The famine was also handled very badly by the government, whose commitment to laissez-faire economics would permit it to do little to alleviate starvation for fear of discouraging individual initiative by creating dependence on government assistance. The famine was an event of unmitigated horror to add to the accumulated miseries already stored in Irish memories, and to many in Ireland the British government and British absentee landlords were responsible for the starvation, not an abstract economic theory, overpopulation, or the natural vicissitudes of potato farming.

Despite its enormous horror, the famine actually had a purgative effect in Ireland because it accelerated certain trends that had started to become evident some years before, including a decline in the rate of population growth, emigration, and land consolidation.[3] Most important, the famine led to a precipitous drop of about 2,225,000 in the Irish population in the years between 1845 and 1851. A million or so people died of hunger and disease, most of them living on subsistence farms, and about 1.5 million emigrated, nearly double the already high rate of emigration that might have been anticipated without the famine. Indeed, high rates of emigration to Britain, the U.S.A., Canada, and Australia continued for the rest of the century so that Ireland's population declined to about 4 million by 1900.

The reduction in population facilitated a reconstruction of the Irish economy based on the halving of the the number of smallest farms, those under five acres, and the expansion of larger farms, those over thirty acres. This action in turn led to an expansion in commercial agriculture, the growth of prosperity in towns across the country, and a general modernization of the Irish economy. Great poverty continued, particularly in the west, where a great deal of subsistence agriculture took place, and many large landlords went bankrupt when their rents disappeared in the famine. The net result, however, was beneficial for the economy.

The famine also created the social bases for Irish nationalism. Irish nationalists might insist that emigration was a tragedy caused by British misgovernment, but as Kerby Miller, a historian of emigration, points out, there were Catholics at the time who recognized "that only massive lower class emigration . . . created the relatively commercialised, urbanized, and bourgeoisie-dominated 'New Ireland,' which had been the precondition for the success of disciplined nationalist movements and the church's devotional revolution. . . ."[4]

As Ireland was changing demographically it was changing in other ways too. Karl Deutsch argues that a nation can be defined as a system of social communication. It is a group of people linked by complementary habits and facilities of communication.[5] A nation has to become self aware to be a nation, which requires its people to break away from old identifications, either with an imperial state or local communities, and its self-conscious existence can be measured by the degree to which it develops a distinctive system of social communications. In late nineteenth-century Ireland, the growth in the sense of an Irish national identity was made possible by improvements in roads, the introduction of the railway network, the population's growing literacy in English, which was the product of a national school system that doubled between 1850 and 1900, and a flourishing national and local press. Mac Laughlin points out that the number of Irish daily newspapers grew from three in 1831 to nineteen in 1887.[6] He also notes that these changes affected both Catholics and northern Protestants, but in opposite ways. Social change was producing two communities in Ireland.

Notwithstanding the growing self-consciousness of two communities in Ireland, Catholic and Protestant, we have to recognize that there were many Protestants who shared the national aspirations of the Irish Catholic community. Some of these, Isaac Butt, Charles Stewart Parnell, and Douglas Hyde, particularly, became outstanding nationalist leaders, but they were too few in number for it to be argued that Irish nationalism was ecumenical and represented both communities. These Protestants had, as it were, left their own community to join the other side.

NATIONALISM IN THE NINETEENTH CENTURY

As Irish society was being reshaped in the second half of the nineteenth century, nationalism as we know it today was being born in Europe. As a movement and an ideology, Irish nationalism literally could not have existed before the second half of the nineteenth century even though a sense of Irish cultural identity undoubtedly existed earlier. To understand this assertion we have to consider how nationalism evolved.

In medieval Europe the mass of the people identified with, and owed their primary loyalties to, two bodies, the Roman Catholic Church and their local communities and lords. The state was relatively weak and feudal monarchs depended on the goodwill and support of local lords for their revenues and military power. As this world disintegrated, after about 1500, modern states began to emerge with powerful central governments as their most distinguishing features. These states became very important objects of loyalty and service for citizens, and the Roman Catholic Church lost much of its ability to intrude in the affairs of states, even Catholic states that had not participated in the Protestant Reformation in the sixteenth century.

In Europe, the Treaty of Westphalia, 1648, symbolically recognized something that had been evolving for several centuries, that highly centralized sovereign states were the undisputed primary actors in European international relations. A new relationship evolved between the people and these new states that was one foundation of modern nationalism. One could begin to talk of the people of the state as "the nation" in the sense that the nation was the body of a state's citizens. This concept grew in importance in the periods of the American and French revolutions at the end of the eighteenth century when democratic theory asserted that to be legitimate a state had to be properly constituted. In other words, the authority of the state had to flow from its citizens, or the nation.

At first the nation was defined in civic and geographical terms. It was composed of citizens who lived within the territory of a state and were loyal to its institutions, even if they spoke several languages and worshiped in a variety of ways. These have been called "civic" or "territorial nations"—what the American nation is today. In the nineteenth century, however, the nation came to be seen differently in much of Europe, as an ethnic community. An *ethnie*, to use the French term, is a group of people who share a common identity that is deeply rooted in some combination of characteristics: a distinctive language or religion; a culture, with distinctive music, literature, and folklore; a physical or racial type; or an attachment to a historic homeland. Most important, an ethnie is made up of people who have shared memories, particularly of their oppression by some dominant group. By this definition several ethnic nations might live in a single state, as was the case in Austria-Hungary before 1919, or several states might share a single nation, as they had in central Europe where many ethnic German states existed before German unification in 1870. It also came to be argued in the second half of the nineteenth century that ethnic nations should be states, and that states should be ethnic nations. In other words, the ideal form of social and political organization was the nation-state in which citizens were predominantly of one ethnie. By this principle, nations that were not yet states had a moral and democratic right to become states: they had the right to break away to form new states or to incorporate co-nationals living in different states into one state. This was known as the right of national self-determination.

In Italy and Germany in the nineteenth century national self-determination was an integrating force because a number of states sharing a single ethnic identity were unified in a single nation-state, Italy in 1861 and Germany in 1871. Elsewhere, in the Austro-Hungarian and Turkish Empires and in the United Kingdom after the emergence of Irish nationalism, national self-determination was disintegrative because it led ethnic nations to demand the right to secede from states. As historian Alfred Cobban noted of national self-determination, "Its logical consequence was that any state which could not persuade its people to regard themselves as a single national community, and so become a nation state, must lose its cohesion, and its diverse elements fly apart."[7]

Whether integrative or disintegrative, national self-determination was profoundly destabilizing in nineteenth century Europe where many states were multinational, including the United Kingdom. In effect, national self-determination required the substantial reconstruction of the political map of Europe, as actually happened in the Austro-Hungarian empire when it lost World War I and was broken up into a number of new states. Established states were determined to resist this process of deconstruction, but even if they accepted it, or it could be imposed on them, as it was on Austria-Hungary in 1919, national self-determination was always very hard to accomplish. The main problem was that populations in many parts of Europe had become intermixed to such a degree that it was almost impossible to draw a new map of Europe which did not find sizeable ethnic minorities trapped inside territories claimed for statehood by nationalists.

This intermixing of ethnic nations was particularly evident in eastern Europe, in the territories of the Ottoman and Austro-Hungarian empires, but it was evident in the United Kingdom too, and especially in Ireland. Had an Irish state been established in 1900 for the whole of Ireland, for example, it would have included a Catholic nationalist majority of 75 percent and a Protestant unionist minority of 25 percent. As it was, after the partition of Ireland by the United Kingdom in 1921, the ostensibly Catholic south had a Protestant minority of 10 percent and the ostensibly Protestant Northern Ireland had a Catholic minority of nearly 40 percent. The proportion of Catholics in the north could have been reduced by astute boundary drawing but a substantial Catholic minority would always have remained there because a great many Catholics lived in areas of Northern Ireland that were surrounded by Protestants, as in the city of Belfast, where one-third of the population was Catholic.

A. D. Smith has argued that nationalism can be both a political ideology and a political movement.[8] In politics an ideology is a set of beliefs and values that protect or promote a preferred political order. In the ideology of ethnic nationalism, the preferred political order is the nation-state, a state based upon a single ethnic group. As a political movement, nationalism is organized to demand national self-determination and the creation of a nation state for the group

The ideology of nationalism was developed by a number of European nationalist movements in the second half of the nineteenth century. In each case, it was predicated on the existence of an ethnie, an ethnic community with distinctive characteristics, particularly a shared language and an attachment to a homeland. What each nineteenth-century nationalist movement did was use ethnic characteristics to create a conscious sense of ethnic nation. In this transformation, as Benedict Anderson, an anthropologist, puts it, the nation was "imagined."[9] Historian Eric Hobsbawm suggests in a similar way that the nineteenth-century European nation was "invented."[10] In his view, people have to be able to imagine a nation before they can consciously be one, and this is the educational task of the nationalist movement.

In much of Europe, with the exception of old states in which a sense of nationhood evolved slowly over time, as in England, the process of building a national identity occurred very quickly and quite recently. European nationalists, including the Irish, began to identify and idealize ethnic homelands as sacred places, with national heroes of mythical proportions. Nationalists searched for distinctive ethnic folklores in poetry, ballads, music, and dance, which they began to teach anew. They produced new art using folklore themes, and they introduced traditional images and symbols into crafts and design. They also wrote new, national histories. In Ireland, this process of "inventing" the past is known as "romantic nationalism."

The new ethnic histories of the nineteenth century were particularly interesting. In real life, history is a very muddled affair, full of contradictions and ambiguities, but nationalists simplified it, intentionally sharpening the divisions between each ethnie and its perceived or actual oppressors. In Ireland, for example, the story of Brian Boru and the battle of Clontarf in 1014 was romantically recreated as a clash between native Irish and Viking invaders, which the Irish won, although the reality is more complex. By 1014 the Vikings had lived in Ireland for two hundred years and were substantially assimilated into the native Irish. This illustrates the fact that though loosely rooted in real events, nationalist histories are frequently mythical. St. Patrick, the fifth-century patron saint of Ireland, was a real person, but is best known by legend and myth, and the same is true of Queen Maeve, Fionn mac Cumhail, and any number of Irish folk heroes. Myths were critically important to nineteenth-century nationalism because, as Jim Mac Laughlin writes, "Myths, especially mythical histories, allowed the Irish to 'reclaim' Ireland."[11]

Who were the nationalists who created nineteenth century ethnic nations? They were predominantly middle-class intellectuals who took leadership roles in nationalist organizations of various kinds or did the research and writing that led to the nationalist rediscovery—or invention—of the past. In the next chapter we will examine who these leaders were in Ireland. They did not act alone because their message had to be spread, and political geographer Jim Mac Laughlin borrows a term from the Italian sociologist, Antonio Gramsci, to call the carriers of the message, the "organic intelligentsia," people with deep roots in ethnic communities who had the training, experience, and/or social status to spread the concept of the ethnic nation.[12] In Catholic Ireland these people were usually from the middle class: the schoolteachers, priests, nuns, publishers, journalists, local politicians, and shopkeepers who were the primary agents in the Irish social communications network of the late nineteenth century. A similar nationalist leadership and organic intelligentsia developed in Protestant Ulster, leading in quite another direction.

CONCLUSION

A. D. Smith suggests that the process of conscious nation-building just described can be evaluated in four dimensions: political, social, cultural, and symbolic.[13] When we analyze these dimensions in Ireland's evolution we will find them expressed in several forms of Catholic nationalism.

According to Smith, in its political dimension, a successful nationalist movement must create an effective political movement, with a core of dedicated and talented leaders, and in its social dimension, it must mobilize substantial popular support. Before the Easter Rising, these two activities, political and social, were pre-eminently the work of constitutional nationalism, which advocated constitutional and political means, not revolution, to achieve a measure of Irish self-government.

Smith next argues that in its cultural dimension, a successful nationalist movement must inculcate the sense that the ethnic group has a distinctive identity and culture. To use a phrase from modern feminism, it must engage in consciousness raising. And finally, in its symbolic dimension, a nationalist movement must promote popular veneration for the symbols of the historic nation, particularly its heroes and martyrs. Smith says the nation must be "a religion surrogate," something worth dying for. These two activities, cultural and symbolic, were largely the work of romantic nationalism, the movement that sought to revive, or invent, a distinctive Irish history and culture. However, yet another kind of Catholic nationalism, revolutionary nationalism, drew upon the culture and symbols generated by romantic nationalism to justify the Easter Rising in 1916.

In the chapters that follow we will the explore the contributions of these different kinds of Catholic Irish nationalism: constitutional, romantic, and revolutionary. We will also consider the special character of Irish nationalism in America and the response of Irish Protestants to the growth of Catholic nationalism.

---

1 Emmet Larkin, "The Devotional Revolution in Ireland, 1850–1875," *American Historical Review*, v. 77, no. 3, (June 1972), pp. 625–52.

2 Foster, p. 219.

3 Ibid., pp. 318–344.
4 Kerby A. Miller, *Emigrants and Exiles: Ireland and the Irish Exodus to North America* (New York, 1985), p. 458.
5 Karl Deutsch, *Nationalism and Social Communication*, 2d ed., (Cambridge, MA), p. 96.
6 Mac Laughlin, pp. 202–207.
7 Alfred Cobban, *The Nation State and National Self-Determination* (London, 1969), p. 42.
8 Anthony D. Smith, ed., *Nationalist Movements* (New York, 1976), Chap. 1.
9 Benedict Anderson, *Imagined Communities* (London, 1991).
10 Eric Hobsbawm and Terence Ranger, eds., *The Invention of Tradition* (New York, 1983), pp. 13–14.
11 Mac Laughlin, p. 143.
12 Ibid., p. 3.
13 Smith, pp. 8–9.

CHAPTER 4

Constitutional Nationalism

THE FIRST THING TO NOTE ABOUT IRISH NATIONALISM in the nineteenth century is that Catholics were not united in a single nationalist movement. As was mentioned briefly in Chapter 3, there were actually three distinct Catholic nationalisms, constitutional, romantic, and revolutionary. They had overlapping objectives and memberships but were distinct categories nonetheless. Only two of them, the revolutionary and romantic forms, were represented in the 1916 Easter Rising, but it was the third, constitutional nationalism, that dominated the Irish scene when World War I broke out in 1914. No one at that time could have predicted with confidence that revolutionary and romantic nationalism would be as important as they were to become, or that they would eclipse constitutional nationalism in the Irish popular imagination.

Constitutional nationalism was never fully mature in the sense of Smith's model of development presented in Chapter 3, with its political, social, cultural, and symbolic components. The constitutionalists certainly satisfied the political and social categories. They had an extraordinarily well-developed political organization, one of the best political party organizations in the world in its day, with adequate funding and a core of dedicated and talented leaders. Also, they mobilized enormous popular support, which was evident in their election successes. By the mid-1880s, there were constitutional nationalist members of Parliament in every majority Catholic district in Ireland. But constitutionalists were relatively unconcerned with Smith's other categories. They did not concern themselves with cultivating a distinctive Irish national culture, nor did they attach much importance to nationalist symbols—these were much better understood by romantic and revolutionary nationalists.

Constitutional nationalism refers to the nationalist movement that sought a measure of self-government for Ireland by constitutional means, through parliamentary pressure and legislation rather than by revolution. Constitutional nationalists drew their inspiration from the Irish Parliament which had existed in Dublin for over five hundred years until the union. That Parliament never attained full independence from Britain, but its existence bore witness to the fact that Ireland was a separate political community for many centuries, even though the two countries shared one monarch. Furthermore, the union that began in 1801 was a very muddled affair in practice and by any measure Ireland continued to be abysmally governed, which quickly provoked the justified hostility of Irish politicians, particularly Catholics, who began to look for alternatives.

THE GOVERNMENT OF IRELAND AFTER THE UNION

When Ireland was integrated into the United Kingdom in 1801 it was assigned 100 seats in the House of Commons, a number later rising to 105, and 32 seats in the House of Lords. But it retained a separate system of administration from that in Britain, almost as if it were a British colony. A viceroy, the lord lieutenant, remained in Ireland to represent the Crown, and he presided over a royal court in Dublin Castle. The chief secretary for Ireland, a member of the U.K. government, worked from London but half of the government departments operating in Ireland were controlled from Dublin, by a resident under secretary.

A further distinction between the governments of Britain and Ireland was that Parliament frequently passed different laws for the two countries on rural distress, local government, transport, land reform, elections, and much more. Indeed, a huge amount of parliamentary time was taken up with Irish business. The most important differences in laws concerned public order in Ireland. Brian Jenkins writes, "In contrast to those in Great Britain, the rural disturbances in Ireland were persistent, extensive, destructive, and savage. The smaller island seemed to be forever teetering on the brink of anarchy."[1] Coercion legislation to control violence was continually being invoked in Ireland, and it was the problem of public order, more than any other, that kept a separate Irish administration in place. The lord lieutenant had very broad powers to deal with unrest, including control of the army in Ireland.

DANIEL O'CONNELL AND CATHOLIC EMANCIPATION

Quite naturally, Irish political leaders who were impressed by Britain's record of bad government set their sights on the repeal of the Act of Union and the reintroduction of some form of Irish self-government, but first there was an even more important issue to deal with, Catholic emancipation. The penal laws had largely been abandoned in the last quarter of the eighteenth century, but Catholics were still denied the right to sit in Parliament, to be appointed to the judiciary, or to reach the highest ranks in the military or the civil service. Judicial, military, and senior administrative offices were still a Protestant monopoly in the United Kingdom, particularly in Ireland, where the lord lieutenant commanded enormous patronage. Two Catholic emancipation bills were passed by the House of Commons, in 1821 and 1825, but were defeated in the House of Lords. In 1823, Daniel O'Connell, a prominent County Kerry lawyer, created the Catholic Association in Ireland to challenge this continuing discrimination. Two years later the association developed a fundraising technique that mobilized large sums of money for the cause. Full membership cost one guinea a year, but the poor could become associate members for one shilling, payable at the church door in monthly installments of one penny.

In 1828 O'Connell demonstrated the power of his association by defeating a member of the government, C. E. Vesey Fitzgerald, in an election for a parliamentary seat in County Clare. As a Catholic, O'Connell could not take the seat, but with a plentiful supply of funds, the endorsement of the Catholic Church, and the support of millions of Catholics in Ireland and Britain, he was able to mount a great campaign that intimidated the government of the prime minister, the duke of Wellington, into conceding Catholic emancipation in 1829.

The Catholic Association was in many respects a forerunner of modern political parties. It was centrally controlled and very well funded. It endorsed parliamentary candidates and withdrew this support—and the certainty of reelection in many districts—if a candidate, once elected, broke his pledge to support emancipation. The government retaliated petulantly by banning the Catholic Association and restricting the Irish right to vote, from an already limited 216,000 people to just 37,000 of the wealthiest, mainly Protestant, citizens. But the principle of political rights for Catholics had been won, and O'Connell had demonstrated that the hitherto passive Irish masses could be mobilized, a harbinger of things to come. Ireland could now elect members of Parliament who were committed to the repeal of the union, although this was going to be difficult so long as the franchise was restricted to the wealthy.

Once in Parliament, O'Connell found that he had no support for repealing the union among British M.P.s and only a minority of the one hundred Irish members were committed to his movement: thirty-nine repealers in 1832, thirty-four in 1835, and eighteen in 1841. The remaining Irish members were elected by well-to-do voters who supported the status quo. Indeed, as late as 1859, eighty-seven Irish M.P.s were landlords, most of them Protestants.[2] In 1834 O'Connell's motion that asked simply for a committee to consider the effects of the union in Ireland was defeated in the House of Commons by 529 votes to 38. In 1840, therefore, optimistic that his victory in 1829 could be repeated, O'Connell revived the notion of the great campaign. He modeled a Repeal Association on the Catholic Association and set about campaigning for repeal. In 1843 he launched the "Repeal Year." Huge meetings were held in Ireland, several with more than half a million people attending, but in October the government banned a planned meeting at Clontarf, a Dublin suburb, and arrested O'Connell and six leaders of the new Young Ireland movement for conspiracy. Their subsequent convictions were quashed on appeal but the government had managed to stall repeal.

The Repeal Association had 2 million members, and O'Connell clearly had the support of the Catholic masses, but his brand of nationalism was beset by problems. As we have seen, the restrictive franchise prevented the majority of Catholics from voting so antirepealers outnumbered repealers in the Irish delegation to the House of Commons. In Ireland a strong group of Catholic bishops suspected that O'Connell was too radical, but the Young Ireland movement, of which we will learn more in Chapter 5, accused him of not being radical enough, with some justification. O'Connell talked about repeal, which many took to mean a return to the independent Irish Parliament of 1782 to 1800, but that is not what he had in mind. He was a loyal supporter of Queen Victoria and wanted Ireland to remain in the British Empire. By repeal he meant that the Act of Union should be repealed so that a new constitutional relationship between Britain and Ireland could be worked out. His preference was for a federal constitution in which Ireland would be a self-governing province of the U.K., much like an American state, with a parliament of its own.[3]

O'Connell's version of repeal, though moderate, had very little support in Parliament. Indeed, it was not even understood by most British members. They assumed he wanted Irish independence, which would be a threat to the integrity of the British Empire. They were also horrified at the prospect of a Catholic-dominated Irish Parliament because Britain was a country with extremely strong anti-Catholic, or "no popery," sentiments. The Irish were stereotyped in much of the British popular press as lazy, dirty, drunken, violent, and priest-ridden. Many in Britain believed that the source of Ireland's problems was the debased character of its people, not British imperialism or absentee landlords. Daniel O'Connell, who received a substantial allowance from the Repeal Association, was represented as a swindler lining his pockets with the penny-a-month "repeal rents."

In 1845 the repeal movement was still alive, but far from successful, when it was overtaken by events: the onset of the great famine in the fall of 1845. The famine was accompanied by agrarian violence directed by desperate tenant farmers against landowners and by government coercion designed to curb the violence. O'Connell was also attacked as too moderate by supporters of Young Ireland, as we shall see. In 1847, in the middle of the famine crisis, O'Connell died, and the following year his parliamentary organization, by then numbering only thirty-nine M.P.s, was dissolved.

O'Connell has entered the pantheon of Irish nationalist heroes as "the great liberator," but what is generally unacknowledged in the nationalist version of Irish history is that his plan for Irish self-government did not include independence. Indeed, O'Connell may be the least understood figure in modern Irish history. His ability to create a mass organization and a parliamentary party, and his belief that Irish self-government was compatible with Ireland's membership in the United Kingdom, set the precedent for the home rule movement that was to follow, but what resonated with the Catholic masses and nationalist historians was his use of the word "repeal." As one of his biographers, Charles Chevenix Trench, writes, "To the vast majority of those who thronged to his mass meetings, repeal meant driving the Saxon into the sea and taking back the lands of Ireland."[4] That was not at all what O'Connell believed.

HOME RULE

There was no major Irish constitutional nationalist agitation again until 1870 when Isaac Butt, a Protestant member of Parliament, formed the Home Government Association in Dublin. Like O'Connell, Butt was not a doctrinaire separatist. He was actually a conservative who believed in Irish self-government because Ireland was very badly governed from London, not because it was the right of an ethnic nation. In addition, he believed that the exploitation of Catholic tenants by absentee British landlords was provoking a threat to stability and property in Ireland.

Like O'Connell, too, Butt favored self-government, not independence. He asked for an arrangement in which an Irish Parliament, and possibly regional parliaments for England, Scotland, and Wales, would receive their powers from the United Kingdom Parliament in London and be subordinate to that body. This principle became known as "home rule" and the home rule movement became the most significant political force in Ireland until the Easter Rising in 1916. Butt formed a Home Government Association which was transformed into a mass movement, the Home Rule League, in 1873, and the organization soon adopted the fundraising and membership techniques of O'Connell's Catholic and Repeal Associations. In 1874 fifty-nine home rule Irish nationalists, a majority of the Irish members, were elected to Parliament, and the Irish parliamentary party was formed with Butt as chairman.

Earlier attempts to found an independent Irish Party, by O'Connell in the 1830s and by Charles Gavan Duffy in the 1850s, had failed. Butt's new party succeeded in large part because Charles Stewart Parnell, a Protestant M.P. from Meath and the son of a liberal landowner, took over as leader of the party and the Home Rule League in 1880, after Butt's death the year before. The two men had disagreed strongly over tactics, Butt favoring a single-issue campaign based on home rule and Parnell preferring to tie home rule to land reforms. Butt also opposed the way Parnell and others deliberately obstructed business in the House of Commons by an astute use of parliamentary rules to force the government to deal with the Irish problem. Butt preferred a policy of moderation and conciliation in order to win Protestant landlords to the home rule movement, but Parnell was prepared to alienate Protestants by supporting Catholic tenant farmers and being much more aggressive in Parliament.

Parnell expanded the base of the home rule movement and secured new sources of funds from emigrant communities abroad, particularly the United States, the birthplace of his mother. In 1880, for example, he visited and raised £20,000 for the Irish party. From then on, the Irish in America became the most important source of financial support for constitutional nationalism, and the Irish party was able to pay subsistence allowances for many of its members.

Funding sources were essential, of course, but linking home rule to land reform, which was the dominant political issue of the day for Irish Catholics, and to the Catholic Church were actually the keys to Parnell's success. The great majority of Catholic farmers were tenants of Protestant landowners, many of them absentees living in Britain. These tenants had long suffered from an exploitative land-tenure system which, by custom, was not practiced in largely Protestant Ulster. If tenant farmers improved their farms through hard work and investment, the landlords could charge higher rents on the renewal of leases. Furthermore, tenants could be evicted without compensation for their improvements. Since the eighteenth century, the Irish countryside had been the scene of organized violence by secret societies directed against landlords and agents who abused this system. The population explosion in the early nineteenth century had exacerbated the problem as holdings were subdivided time and again down to barely workable plots of five acres or less, but famine deaths drastically cut the population pressure on the land. Farming became more prosperous until bad harvests between 1877 and 1879 revived the agrarian unrest of the past.

Catholic tenant farmers were first mobilized politically by Daniel O'Connell in the 1820s, but by the 1870s the number of substantial Catholic farmers was much larger, and Parnell was able to tie them to constitutional nationalism. In 1879 he helped Michael Davitt found the National Land League. Davitt was a former revolutionary who had returned to Ireland from exile in America. Parnell became president of the organization, and thereby tied the Irish party to the land agitation. After the Land League was banned by the government, its successor, the Irish National League, founded in 1882, became the popular arm of constitutional nationalism in virtually every Catholic parish in Ireland.

Roy Foster says that Parnell's involvement with Davitt's land reform "meant riding a tiger," because Davitt operated in the middle ground between constitutional agitation and agrarian violence.[5] The land league demanded legislation to guarantee fair rents, security of tenure, and the right of a tenant to sell his tenancy for the value of his improvements, but it also organized boycotts, named after Captain Boycott, a land agent in County Mayo, which often overflowed into violence directed against landlords and farmers who took over the farms of evicted tenants. It followed the policy outlined by James Fintan Lalor, who had argued in the 1840s that civil disobedience and nonpayment of rents would destroy Irish landlordism. Landlords, the Land League, and the police were soon involved in violent disputes throughout the country. In effect, Ireland was in a land war from 1879 to 1882.

In 1881, a general election returned sixty-one home rule M.P.s to Parliament. It also returned the Liberal party and William Gladstone to govern the U.K. Gladstone's earlier government (1868–74) had tried to discourage Irish nationalism by legislating several Irish reforms, notably the disestablishment of the Anglican Church of Ireland in 1869 and an ineffective Irish Land Act in 1870.

Gladstone's return to office in 1881 meant that Parnell would be dealing with a man who had shown some sympathy for Ireland in the past, but their relationship was not immediately satisfactory. Gladstone's 1881 Land Act enacted most of the demands of the Land League, but Parnell rejected it because it neglected the serious problem of arrears of rent owed by thousands of farmers. The government banned the league that year for its campaign of intimidation, and Parnell himself was imprisoned in Kilmainham Prison, Dublin, for his role in the movement. After the so-called Kilmainham Treaty between Parnell and Gladstone in 1882, Parnell was released. He agreed to support the Land Act and Gladstone agreed to amend it to pay arrears of rent so that these farmers could benefit from its terms. Parnell also agreed that the Irish party would support the Liberal government. This did not completely end the land agitation, because rents were subsequently withheld again between 1886 and 1889 in the so-called Plan of Campaign, which targeted high rents, but it cemented the relationship between land reform and constitutional nationalism and laid the groundwork for the long-term alliance with the Liberals.

On his release from prison, Parnell, now a hero in Ireland, reorganized the home rule movement and managed to come to terms with the Catholic Church. The majority of Irish bishops had opposed the radical Land League, and Cardinal Cullen of Dublin had long used his power to hamper an independent Irish party, preferring to work with the Liberals, but he struck a deal with Parnell between 1884 and 1886. The church would endorse the Irish party, home rule, and a plan of land purchase for tenant farmers if the party would support the proposition that the education of Catholics, at every level, should be controlled by the church.

In 1885 the Irish party, frustrated by Gladstone's inaction on Irish home rule, forced him out of office by voting with the Conservatives in the House of Commons, and at the subsequent general election, eighty-five home rule M.P.s were elected in Ireland and one in Liverpool, T. P. O'Connor. The full effects of successive extensions of the franchise to include more and more Catholics were felt in this election as Catholic voters took permanent political control of Catholic Ireland and the Liberal party effectively disappeared. Furthermore, Irish home rule M.P.s now held the balance in the House of Commons. The Liberals had an eighty-six-seat margin over the Conservatives but could only form a government if the Irish would support them and not the Conservatives. Parnell had under his command the first modern, disciplined party in parliamentary history, an awesome weapon, and in December 1885 he threw his support to Gladstone who agreed to introduce Irish home rule substantially as Parnell conceived it. The first home rule bill was introduced in April 1886.

The home rule bill will be considered in some detail in Chapter 6, but for the moment we must recognize Parnell's huge achievement. Though a Protestant himself, he had succeeded in organizing the members of Parliament from Catholic Ireland into a highly disciplined and aggressive party. By linking home rule and land reform he had ensured the support of Catholic tenant farmers, the most important social class in Catholic Ireland, and he had built a grass-roots political network with millions of supporters. His was the political party of the Catholic "organic intelligentsia" identified in Chapter 3: the farmers, schoolteachers, priests, nuns, shopkeepers, publishers, and journalists of Catholic Ireland. Finally, Parnell had firmly established a relationship between constitutional nationalism and the church and had sown the seeds for what was to become a Catholic Irish state less than forty years later. "By 1886," writes Emmet Larkin, "the British state had lost the great game it had played for so many centuries in Ireland. An Irish state had not only been created in the minds of most Irishmen, but the national and local political apparatus necessary to the functioning of that state was operative."[6] The 1886 home rule bill, which demonstrated that the hitherto sacrosanct union with Britain was now negotiable, meant that the ratification of some form of Irish state by the U.K. Parliament appeared to be only a matter of time.

Parnell had achieved this success by political organization in Ireland and party discipline in the House of Commons, but always lurking in the background was the threat of violence. The Land League had intimidated the government into concessions and might be mobilized again. In addition, revolutionary nationalists in Ireland and America had realized that Parnell was so dominant a leader that they had no choice but to support him. The "New Departure" policy of 1879, for example, involved an alliance between Parnell, Michael Davitt of the

Land League, and John Devoy of the revolutionary Clan na Gael in America. Although Parnell was not a revolutionary himself, he had the support of men much more violent than he. This fact formed a constant, and rather menacing, backdrop to his negotiations with the Liberals.

The home rule movement that Parnell built survived until World War I, winning the support of the mass of Irish Catholic voters and consistently sending more than eighty home rule members to Parliament. It achieved this despite a great leadership crisis in 1890 after the husband of Parnell's mistress, Katherine O'Shea, cited Parnell as corespondent in his divorce suit. It was a measure of Parnell's enormous stature in the movement that he was not immediately denounced by his followers, most of whom were Catholics; and it was a measure of his poor judgment in the case that he clung to leadership and refused to resign. His defeat was finally forced when Gladstone repudiated him. The Irish party then divided on the issue. Two-thirds of the party rejected Parnell and installed Justin McCarthy as the parliamentary leader. The minority, loyal to Parnell and resentful of Gladstone's interference, followed John Redmond. Parnell himself contracted rheumatic fever during a campaign to reassert his position in Ireland and died in October 1891.

Parnell's death did not heal the rift in the party, and it was not until 1900 that the factions came together again. A new popular organization founded in 1898, the United Irish League, became the medium for the reconciliation. It saw the majority anti-Parnellite leader, John Dillon, generously yielding to the Parnellite John Redmond as leader of both the Irish party and the new league. The reunion was extremely successful, and it is not true, as historian George Dangerfield asserted, that Parnell took home rule with him to the grave, from which it emerged only briefly in 1912.[7] The parliamentary agitation was actually far from dead. The Irish had always depended on a favorable distribution of power in the House of Commons for their parliamentary victories, and when this distribution occurred again after an election in 1910, they were prepared. In the intervening years, as a parliamentary party, as a mass movement in Ireland and America, and with renewed financial support from the United States, constitutional nationalism marched confidently towards what it regarded as the certain victory of home rule, virtually unchallenged by the revolutionaries who took the field in 1916.

Hand in hand with its progress in the field of party politics, constitutional nationalism was making giant strides in the Irish administration, particularly after the return of a Liberal government in 1906. When Parnell became leader of the movement in 1880, there was only one Catholic among forty-one heads of government departments in Ireland. By 1914 more than half of the by then forty-eight departments were headed by Catholics or Protestant supporters of home rule, and there was an equal division of Catholics and Protestants in the Irish Supreme Court. Ireland was no longer a unionist dictatorship. The administration for an Irish state was already established.

Conclusion

Political scientist Jack Snyder, writing on ethnic nationalism, recognizes that it is rooted in ethnic differences but denies that most nationalist conflicts are rooted in "ancient hatreds." Instead, in the early periods of democratization and modernization, nationalists use new political freedoms or resources to mobilize popular support for interests they want to promote.[8] In Ireland, the expansion of the franchise in six reform acts in the nineteenth century and the development of a social communications network, the provincial press, roads, railways, and so on in the second half of the nineteenth century, represented the democratization and modernization that allowed the constitutional nationalists to mobilize Irish nationalism in support of several interests. Nationalism served the interests of Irish politicians who wanted opportunities to shape Irish policy in Dublin that they could never hope to gain in London. It also served the interests of the Catholic Church. At the very least the church saw Irish self-government as a way for it to gain control of the education of Irish Catholics, but there was a broader agenda which became clear when Irish nationalists gained control of an independent Ireland in 1922. The church quickly came to assert an extraordinary power in the public life of Ireland, influencing not only education but the laws of censorship, marriage, divorce, public health and reproductive rights, all of which would have been different if Ireland had continued to be governed from London.

Irish nationalism particularly served the interests of Catholic tenant farmers, who had grown in number and strength since the famine in the 1840s. Emmet Larkin defines tenant farmers holding more than thirty acres as the "nation forming class."[9] They had substantial grievances against their landowners, many of them absentees in Britain, and they also had legitimate fears for the security of their holdings. They wanted land reform, and although the Liberal, Gladstone, moved to satisfy some of their demands in 1881, and Conservative government reforms of 1903 and 1909 allowed most farmers to buy the land they had rented, these developments came too late, much as local government reform came too late in 1898 to stop the demand for Irish self-government. By the last quarter of the nineteenth century, constitutional nationalism was already firmly entrenched in the Catholic community.

Constitutional nationalism was a great success, therefore, and two men were particularly responsible, Charles Stewart Parnell and John Redmond. There were marked differences, however, between their two agitations. Though Redmond was a competent leader, he did not inspire a following, and although Parnell, by all reports, was aloof and distant from his supporters, he managed to create a powerful personal loyalty. More important was the fact that by Redmond's time, constitutional nationalism had divorced itself from incipient violence. The Conservatives' successful Land Act of 1903 had ended agrarian radicalism. Some of the successes of constitutionalism had therefore blunted its cutting edge, which had always been its tacit relationship with the those responsible for rural violence. Parnell knew how to manipulate the threat of violence, but by temperament and circumstance, Redmond was incapable of doing so. As historian Oliver MacDonagh suggests, "Redmond was inhibited by his own beliefs from enlisting Irish militancy as an ally."[10] As we shall see in Chapter 8, he paid a heavy price for his sensitivity when a home rule victory was snatched from him by militant Protestant unionists in 1914.

1 Brian Jenkins, *Era of Emancipation: British Government in Ireland, 1812–1830* (Montreal, 1988), p. 38.

2 Foster, p. 377.

3 Alan J. Ward, *The Irish Constitutional Tradition: Responsible Government and Modern Ireland, 1782–1992* (Washington, DC, 1994), pp. 43–45.

4 Charles Chevenix Trench, *The Great Dan: A Biography of Daniel O'Connell* (London, 1984), p. 193.

5 Foster, p. 405.

6 Emmet Larkin, "Church, State, and Nation in Modern Ireland," *American Historical Review* 80: 5 (December 1975), p. 1266.

7 George Dangerfield, *The Damnable Question* (Boston, 1976), p. 23.

8 Jack Snyder, *From Voting to Violence: Democratization and Nationalist Conflict* (New York, 2000), pp. 15–43.

9 Larkin, "Church, State and Nation in Modern Ireland," pp. 1244–1276.

10 Oliver MacDonagh, *Ireland* (Englewood Cliffs, NJ, 1968), p. 57.

CHAPTER 5

Romantic and Revolutionary Nationalism

THE MOMENTUM OF CONSTITUTIONAL NATIONALISM was checked in 1914 for reasons which we will explore in Chapter 6, and the consequence was the Easter Rising two years later. "Checked" is certainly a more appropriate word than "destroyed" because constitutionalism deeply influenced both the political institutions and the political behavior of the independent Ireland that ultimately emerged from the Easter Rising. Nonetheless, it was overshadowed by the revolutionary movement for a while. In this chapter we will examine revolutionary nationalism and its close relation, romantic nationalism, through which a number of revolutionary leaders entered the movement.

ROMANTIC NATIONALISM

In his book, *National Identity*, A. D. Smith, describes the vital contribution that romantic nationalists, whom he describes as intellectuals, make to modern nationalist movements:[1]

> It is the intellectuals—poets, musicians, painters, sculptors, novelists, historians and archeologists, playwrights, philologists, anthropologists and folklorists—who have proposed and elaborated the language and concepts of the nation and nationalism and have, through their musings and research, given voice to wider aspirations that they have conveyed in appropriate images, myths and symbols.[1]

This intellectual activity was critically important in Ireland as it was in much of Europe in the nineteenth century. Whereas the constitutional movement in Ireland was primarily concerned with establishing a regional government in Dublin that would be more responsive to Irish needs than the U.K. government in London, and the revolutionary movement was motivated by a hatred for England, a disdain for constitutional agitation, and a desire for political independence, the romantic movement approached nationalism from the perspective of the national culture. Its purpose was to revive, even to create, a distinctively Irish culture. In terms of Smith's four-part model of development as described earlier, romantic nationalism eschewed political organization and social mobilization as such; but it sought to create a popular awareness of a distinctive Irish culture; and it was critically important in identifying and cultivating nationalist symbols.

In 1842, three founders of the Young Ireland movement, a Protestant, Thomas Davis, and two Catholics, John B. Dillon and Charles Gavan Duffy, began to publish a weekly newspaper, *Nation*, to expound their view that Ireland was a geographical, cultural, and spiritual entity. They attacked the materialism of industrial and commercial England and the introduction of its values into Ireland. The Irish, they argued, possessed a history, heritage, and culture of their own. The *Nation* published Irish prose, poetry, and essays on history, ethnography, and antiquities. It extolled the heroic image of ancient Ireland and urged the restoration of the Irish language, then spoken by less than a quarter of the population. England was accused of having deprived the Irish of their culture, and without a culture, there could be no Irish nation. The purpose of Young Ireland, therefore, was to construct the Irish nation by discovering—modern theorists would say by inventing—the Irish past. Davis, for example, spoke of Ireland as "a nation once again," and of wanting "to inflame and purify" the Irish with a "lofty and heroic love of country."[2] Central to the Young Ireland argument was the proposition that Irish nationality transcends religion and race. Protestants and Catholics were held to be as one in the Irish nation, but the emphasis upon a distant and Gaelic past was bound to divide the two Irish communities, the Gaelic from the non-Gaelic.

The Young Irelanders split from O'Connell's repeal movement in the mid-1840s when they endorsed a nonreligious education system.

They saw sectarianism as divisive and destructive of the unity of the Irish nation, and in this sense they were ecumenical. O'Connell, by contrast, was a politician who was anxious not to alienate the Catholic Church, so he decided to endorse a church education system for Catholics as Parnell did later. Young Irelanders also differed from O'Connell in their attitude towards the Irish language. They argued the need to revive the Irish language, but O'Connell, who spoke Irish himself, insisted that its use would hamper the intellectual and economic development of Ireland. His nationalism was utilitarian not cultural.

In 1847 the Young Irelanders founded the Irish Confederation as a popular organization to challenge O'Connell's Repeal Association, and in 1848 they turned to revolution, albeit reluctantly and abysmally. The *Nation* had consistently praised the warrior heroes of ancient Ireland, but its editors were not, by instinct or aptitude, revolutionaries themselves. Their small rising, in Tipperary, was decisively crushed, but their example entered the folklore of violent resistence to English oppression. Furthermore, and more importantly, the *Nation's* message that Ireland was a cultural and spiritual entity proved to be extraordinarily influential in subsequent years. As McCaffrey argues, "Davis, Dillon and Duffy gave Irish nationalism the most powerful and influential newspaper voice it ever had or ever would have, and they contributed traditions and values that would permanently shape its character."[3]

Romantic nationalism re-emerged in three major examples in the 1880s and 1890s, ironically, just as Ireland's most material grievances were being resolved by reforms in land tenure, local government, and education. The first was the Gaelic Athletic Association (G.A.A.), founded in the west of Ireland by Michael Cusack in 1884. It promoted traditional Irish games and pastimes, such as Gaelic football and hurling, and traditional music and dance, and it forbade its members to play English games, such as soccer or cricket. It became extremely influential in rural Ireland and is still alive and well in the twenty-first century. Most of the important sports and cultural competitions in the Irish Republic today are sponsored by the G.A.A..

The second example of romantic nationalism was the Gaelic League, founded in 1893. It appealed to a different group of people, not those interested in traditional sports and pastimes but members of the middle class, well educated and urban, who wanted to promote the study and practice of the Irish language and literature, each of which had steadily declined over the years. Indeed, by the late nineteenth century Irish was the native language only of peasants in the remote west and southwest of the island. Many of the leaders of 1916, including Patrick Pearse and Eamon de Valera, were introduced to Irish nationalism by the Gaelic League, which had accumulated more than six hundred branches and many thousands of dedicated supporters by 1908. Its influence was so great that by 1910 every student at the National University of Ireland was required to matriculate in Irish.

The third example of Irish romantic nationalism acquired the name, "the Irish literary revival." In the 1890s a group of writers, predominantly Protestant and from the Anglo-Irish upper class, founded a literary movement in the belief that Ireland had suffered from English cultural imperialism and was in need of an indigenous culture. They differed from the Gaelic League in believing that the literary medium could be English, the first language by then of most of the Irish. The movement was associated with the National Literary Society, founded in Dublin in 1892, and the Abbey Theater, founded by W. B. Yeats and Lady Gregory in 1904. It attracted a number of other writers, notably J. M. Synge, G. W. Russell, and George Moore. For inspiration and themes they turned to Irish peasant life, that is to say, to those in Ireland whose culture had been least affected by exposure to England. They also turned to the history, sagas, fairy tales, and oral folklore of Ireland. They drew heavily from the research of Standish O'Grady who, in Dangerfield's phrase, had begun "unlocking one of the richest mythologies in Europe" in the 1880s.[4]

The literary revival attracted writers of international stature and cosmopolitan standards who wanted to create an Irish literature in English from Irish sources, but their work was often controversial. They encountered the hostility of the Catholic hierarchy and many members of the Gaelic League who represented, in the bourgeois view of Yeats and his colleagues, a narrow, parochial, and idealized view of Irish life. The writers were accused of misrepresenting Irish womanhood, of demeaning Irish peasants, of undermining Catholic morals, and of neglecting the Irish language, the very heart of a national culture, although they produced some plays in Irish at the Abbey Theater.

Eager patriots, anxious to protect the reputation of the Irish nation as they saw it from these Anglo-Irish usurpers of Irish traditions, staged protests in 1907, the "Playboy Riots," when the Abbey Theatre staged Synge's play, *The Playboy of the Western World,* which was about a drunken wastrel.

The issue at stake in the protests, in a fundamental sense, was artistic freedom. The church believed that art should be an instrument of religious and moral education, and many nationalists believed it should be an instrument of national propaganda. But Yeats had battled since the 1890s for artistic freedom in Ireland, and he refused to build an Irish literature or an Irish nation on foundations of ignorance or deceit. However, by 1910 he and his colleagues had lost what F. S. L. Lyons calls, "the battle of the two civilizations."[5] The narrow parochialists and moralists came to dominate Irish literature until the 1960s, and some of Ireland's most acclaimed writers, James Joyce, Sean O'Casey, and Samuel Beckett, for example, found that they could only work abroad, though their art was always inspired by their Irishness.

The literary revival was not sustained, but it contributed to a growing sense of national identity and in later years came to be accepted as one of the cultural glories of Ireland. Together with the Gaelic League and the Gaelic Athletic Association, it encouraged the notion that Ireland possessed a culture with traditions and customs quite separate from England.

In one critical respect, as we have already seen, the Gaelic revival differed from the literary revival. Its nationalism was explicitly Gaelic and was tied to the ancient culture of the Catholic majority. Douglas Hyde, one of the founders of the Gaelic League and a Protestant himself, claimed to be nonsectarian, but his determination to make Irish the national language and, in his phrase, to "de-Anglicize" Ireland, had revolutionary implications for the quarter of the nation that claimed it was not Irish in the Gaelic sense. Hyde's was the message of Thomas Davis and Young Ireland, of what came to be known as "Irish Ireland." It was nativistic, meaning that its definition of the nation was exclusive, not inclusive. It did not include what was English and Protestant in Ireland. Rather than seeking a framework which might accommodate all Irish, it excluded, as had the aristocratic Protestant

Irish nation in the eighteenth century, all those who did not conform to its definition of Irish. This exclusive definition alienated the members of the literary revival, most of whom were Anglo-Irish themselves and were therefore separated by birth from its central assumptions.

The irony is that Irish Ireland was never accepted by the majority of the Catholic Irish themselves even when, from the 1920s, the weight of the Irish state and its educational system were thrown into battle. The dream of an Irish culture, whether Gaelic or Anglo-Irish, inspired many Irish men and women who made critically important contributions to the Irish nation, including leaders of the Easter Rising, but Roy Foster reminds us that "the majority Irish culture was not that of the cultural ginger groups, Irish-Irish and Anglo-Irish. It was that of respectable Victorian Ireland. . . ."[6]

From the perspective of the Easter Rising, Patrick Pearse, the commander in chief of the republican forces, was the most distinguished product of the Gaelic revival, and he forged a unique blend of romantic and revolutionary nationalism. In 1908 he founded St. Edna's, a bilingual school in Dublin which stressed Irish language, history, culture, and games. Pearse believed that the educational system imposed on Ireland by England had crushed the Irish national spirit. Liberation could only be achieved by the overthrow of English education, and ultimately by the overthrow of English imperialism. Pearse was greatly influenced by the heroic deed and the heroic image, and at times offered a sacrificial vision in which Ireland could only be reborn by the blood sacrifice of a few. Bloodshed, he argued, "is a cleansing thing and the nation which regards it as the final horror has lost its manhood."[7]

Pearse became an active revolutionary quite late in the day, in 1913, like two other Gaelic League members, Thomas MacDonagh and Joseph Plunkett. All were Gaelic enthusiasts, all were poets, and all believed in the value of self sacrifice. At the Dublin funeral of an old rebel, O'Donovan Rossa (who had died in America), an extraordinary symbolic act manipulated for dramatic effect by the Irish Republican Brotherhood, Pearse declared, "Life springs from death; and from the graves of patriot men and women spring living nations."[8] He could not have had high hopes of defeating the English in battle, although there were moments when he thought it possible. In October 1914 he told an Irish-American fundraiser that money for weapons "may mean victory. Its failure to come may mean either a bloody debacle like '98 or a dreary fizzling out like '48 and '67."[9] However, if military victory were denied as was probable, victory of a kind would still come, as it came for Christ, from his sacrifice and his example. As a character, McDara, says in Pearse's play, *The Singer*, "One man can free a people as one Man redeemed the world."[10] The rebellion would be not a gesture only, but a declaration of Irish independence.

In Pearse, then, was combined the revolutionary impulse of earlier rebels, such as Wolfe Tone and Robert Emmet, the cultural and spiritual vision of the Young Irelanders and the Gaelic League, the commitment to self-sacrifice of a Christian martyr. It proved to be an extraordinarily volatile mixture. The historian of Irish literature, Malcolm Brown, wrote that by the 1840s Irish Nationalists had learned that their opportunities must be made as well as waited for:

> Flaming words, redemptive symbology—these were essential, granted; and Irish modes in religion, language, and cultural tradition had to be collected, arrayed and made battle-ready. But the brother-nationalists of Wales and Scotland had done all that, and still they remained mere dilettantes. They lacked the advanced Irishman's professional respect for the deed.

No cure, Brown added, "was as magical as a bold dramatic action...."[11]

Pearse appreciated this view better than others of his time. A romantic nationalist at heart, his was to be the revolutionary deed. In Pearse, then, we find personified both romantic and revolutionary nationalism.

REVOLUTIONARY NATIONALISM

The Easter Rising was the most important step in Irish revolutionary history, but the revolutionary movement, which committed itself to the liberation of Ireland by force, always represented a small minority of the population. Like its constitutional counterpart, it was never fully mature in the sense of Smith's model of development described at the end of Chapter 3, although in different ways. It attracted dedicated leaders, but they were, for the most part, poor organizers and frequently divided among themselves. As Malcolm Brown says, "Even the warmest friend of Ireland must confess that its revolutionary staff work throughout history was never better than slovenly."[12] One result is that revolutionary nationalism was never a popular mass movement before 1916, and its active supporters were always very few. In addition, while some revolutionary nationalists, particularly the Young Ireland leaders and Patrick Pearse, were concerned with Irish history and culture, this was not a consistent theme in the movement. Most revolutionaries were motivated by hostility toward England rather than any really substantial vision of a new Ireland. As John Mitchel, one of their number, wrote of his fellow revolutionaries, "I have found that there was perhaps less of love than hate. . . ."[13] But the revolutionaries were extremely adept at manipulating symbols, the heroes and martyrs of Irish history, and on special occasions found they could use this skill to mobilize support from large numbers of people whose nationalism was latent or relatively passive, people who generally expressed themselves through the constitutional movement.

Revolutionary nationalism was committed to the establishment by force of an independent Irish republic. England would have to be driven out of Ireland because it would never leave willingly. There had always been native Irish resistence to invasion and oppression but modern revolutionary nationalism can be dated back to the Society of United Irishmen, founded in 1791 by middle-class Protestants who included Wolfe Tone and Robert Emmet. Henry Grattan, who led the agitation for an independent Irish Parliament in 1782, was inspired by the democratic principles of the American Revolution, but the United Irishmen were inspired by the French Revolution and its view of a new society. Their aims were not at first revolutionary, and included Catholic emancipation, universal suffrage, and parliamentary reform, but the character of the movement soon changed. The society became involved with violent, agrarian, secret societies, the Catholic "Defenders," and the Protestant "Peep O'Day Boys," for example, and members began to intrigue with France which was at war with England. The society was forced underground in 1794 after British government informers learned of secret negotiations with the French government.

Wolfe Tone was one of a number of leaders who fled Ireland in 1794. He emigrated, permanently he thought, to the United States, but was given the task of opening negotiations between the United Irishmen and France through its representatives in America. In January 1796 he went to France to encourage and help plan a French invasion of Ireland. The French were led to believe that Ireland was seething with revolution, but in fact the United Irishmen were poorly organized and the uncoordinated agitation in Ireland was primarily concerned with correcting rural grievances, not with Irish independence. Furthermore, agrarian violence often became sectarian violence as the Protestant Peep O'Day Boys, who were reorganized as the Orange Society in 1795, attacked Catholic targets and the Catholic Defenders replied in kind. A coordinated Irish revolution was further inhibited by the Irish Parliament which passed the Insurrection Act of 1796, and the Irish government, which suspended habeas corpus in its zeal to suppress the Defenders. Nevertheless, in December 1796, Wolfe Tone and a fleet of ships carrying fourteen thousand French sailed for Bantry Bay in Ireland. Heavy storms prevented any troop landings, which was fortunate in a way for France because Ireland was not organized for a rebellion, and a spontaneous uprising was out of the question.

A rebellion did occur in May 1798, but it, too, was a failure, developing as a series of uncoordinated actions that were easily and brutally suppressed by early July. Only in Wexford, where it attracted approximately thirty thousand volunteers, was there a significant rising, and even there it was aimless and poorly led. When French troops landed at Killala, County Mayo, in the west of Ireland, in August, they found virtually no revolutionary activity and were captured within weeks. Wolfe Tone himself sailed from France in September 1798 and was captured at sea. He joined about seventy other leaders of the United Irishmen in prison and became a martyr to the cause of Irish freedom when he died, after a suicide attempt, in November 1798.

In 1803 there was another abortive United Irish rising in Dublin. Three thousand volunteers were expected to attack Dublin Castle during the evening of July 23, but only about three hundred turned out, and Robert Emmet led a confused attack which was over within a few hours. As Robert Kee writes, "The plan itself was reasonable and practical, its execution lamentable to the point of farce."[14] But Emmet was martyred by execution. His contribution to the nationalist cause lay primarily in his heroic example and an inspiring speech from the dock which concluded, "When my country takes her place among the nations of the earth, then, and not till then, let my epitaph be written."[15] He joined Wolfe Tone in the Irish revolutionary pantheon.

The United Irishmen were generally Anglo-Irish and, few in number; they mobilized little popular support. Ideologically they were Irish Jacobins, motivated by the democratic and egalitarian ideas of the French revolution rather than the history, culture, and national identity of Ireland, and they had nothing in common with nineteenth-century romantic nationalists. They failed in all they attempted except that they became martyrs for the very different class of Irish nationalists who were responsible for the Easter Rising in 1916.

Revolutionary Irish nationalism was not revived until 1848, the year of revolution in Europe. Its instrument was the Young Ireland movement, which was more distinguished by its contribution to romantic nationalism, as we have seen, than for its revolutionary skill. Young Ireland was associated with O'Connell's repeal agitation in the early 1840s, and it was only after O'Connell's death in 1847 that the revolutionary strain in the movement became dominant, and not for long. John Mitchel, formerly an editor of the Young Ireland newspaper, the *Nation*, led the way. His new paper, the *United Irishman*, which he founded in January 1848, urged that preparations should be made for a revolution. He was soon arrested and sentenced in May 1848 to be transported for a term of fourteen years to Van Dieman's Land, known as Tasmania since 1855, in Australia. He was rescued by an Irish-American expedition in 1853 and moved to the U.S.A.

More arrests of Young Irelanders followed. The *Nation* was suppressed, habeas corpus was suspended, and martial law was imposed in several parts of Ireland. In May 1848 a small Young Ireland rebellion occurred, provoked by government coercion and repression. It was an utter failure; an unplanned revolution, disowned by the Catholic Church, unsupported by the Irish people, and degenerating into farce. The small force led by William Smith O'Brien in County Tipperary was quickly defeated in what was disparagingly, but justifiably, derided as "the battle of the Widow McCormack's cabbage plot."[16]

The Young Irelanders were people of considerable talent who would have formed a distinguished political elite in any country, but after the rebellion they were dispersed around the world. O'Brien, John Martin, T. B. McManus, and Thomas Meagher were transported, like Mitchel, to Australia. McManus and Meagher joined Mitchel by escaping to America where Meagher served as a brigadier general in the Union army in the American Civil War and the commander of an Irish-American brigade, before becoming governor of the Montana territory. Ironically, Mitchel, a fighter for Irish freedom, supported the slaveholder Confederacy. Darcy McGee fled to Canada where he became a minister in the Canadian dominion government before being murdered by an Irish extremist in 1868. James Stephens and John O'Mahony fled to France, and O'Mahony went on to America. Charles Gaven Duffy managed to escape conviction, despite being prosecuted several times. He was at heart a home ruler, not a revolutionary, and he served in the House of Commons in the 1850s, but even he emigrated to Australia. He became prime minister of the colony of Victoria before returning to Ireland as an old man.

Many Young Irelanders were sentenced to death, but the sentences were commuted. The government would not make them martyrs, even if O'Brien did declare that he would refuse clemency. They failed as revolutionaries and certainly failed to mobilize popular opinion, but they made a great contribution in their nonrevolutionary endeavors to romantic nationalism and the definition of an Irish national culture. Although they were not executed, their rebellion and their assorted exiles made them heroes and martyrs of sorts.

For many Young Irelanders, 1848 was a solitary revolutionary fling, but for others it marked a new direction. In 1858, James Stephens founded the Irish Republican Brotherhood (IRB) to work for an independent Irish republic by physical force. In the United States a related organization, the Fenian Brotherhood, from a Gaelic word for soldiers, was founded by another Young Irelander, John O'Mahony. Both organizations came to be known popularly as "the Fenians." Fenianism was distinctive in that it was both Irish and Irish American, and from 1873 the two branches were united by a single revolutionary directorate with seven members. The movement actually had more members in America, where it could operate openly among the enormous number of postfamine immigrants, than it did in Ireland, where it had to operate in secret. In both countries it had primarily a working-class following, and it had considerable support among Irish enlisted in the British army. The members appear to have been motivated primarily by a visceral hatred of England, but there were some with more complex motivations. John O'Leary, for example, a Young Irelander who led the IRB for many years before his death in 1907, was very much a nationalist intellectual. He was an ardent collector of Irish literature and history and had a profound influence on the young W. B. Yeats. As Malcolm Brown argues, "He believed that Irish poetry must be national, and Irish nationalism poetic."[17] Nonetheless, as a whole Fenianism was rather single-minded in its commitment to the establishment of an Irish Republic by revolution.

Fenianism was opposed by constitutional nationalists, by many of the survivors of Young Ireland, and most importantly by the Catholic Church, which condemned its secrecy and feared its radical and revolutionary influence among the poor. The Fenians were, with few exceptions, Catholics themselves but either kept their membership a secret from their priests, withdrew from the church, or found sympathetic priests in whom to confide. The Roman Catholic Church has always opposed secret societies and revolutionary violence in Ireland, but one of the characteristics of revolutionary nationalists, even today, has been their refusal to allow the church hierarchy to influence this part of their lives. The ultimate evidence of their commitment to their country has been their rejection of the church on this one issue, even in the face of excommunication.

Many of the more than one hundred thousand Irish Americans who fought in the American Civil War became Fenians, and some returned to Ireland after the war to participate in a rising, but the British government had informers in the movement on both sides of the Atlantic and intervened several times to forestall action. In September 1865, for example, Jeremiah O'Donovan Rossa, John O'Leary, Charles Kickham, Thomas Luby, and others were arrested in Ireland. In November James Stephens was captured, but he escaped within weeks and fled to America. In February 1866, seven hundred more suspected

Fenians were arrested and imprisoned without trial. John Devoy, who was to lead the revolutionary movement in America for many years and helped to plan the Easter Rising, was imprisoned in Ireland as a Fenian from 1866 to 1871.

The long-anticipated Fenian rising in Ireland did not occur until February and March 1867 when several thousand men, led by an Irish-American, Thomas J. Kelly, attempted risings in Dublin, Cork, Tipperary, and elsewhere. The government suppressed them within a few days, with little loss of life. An American supply ship, *Erin's Hope*, which was to arm them, did not arrive until May. One hundred and sixty Fenians were convicted for their parts in the rising, but again, there were no executions. The government did not want to create Fenian martyrs.

In America, where anti-British sentiment was high after the Civil War, the Fenian Brotherhood had a career which was somewhat more spectacular. It operated more or less openly, with parades and drills. An invasion of Ireland was impossible for the Fenians, but on May 31, 1866, fifteen hundred of them invaded Canada, then a British colony, at Niagara. The invasion was quickly repelled, and two other raids across the border, in 1870 and 1871, were equally aborted.

The Fenian Brotherhood died in America as a revolutionary organization in the early 1870s. The American Catholic Church had joined the Church in Ireland in banning the organization, the American government became less tolerant of Fenian activities as relations with Britain improved in the 1870s, and the Fenian leadership was constantly torn by dissension. The organization was succeeded as the primary Irish revolutionary organization in America by the Clan na Gael, founded in 1867.

To the limited degree that Fenianism survived in Ireland in the IRB, it was as a terrorist organization. For example, Fenians assassinated Lord Frederick Cavendish, the Irish chief secretary, and T. H. Burke, his under secretary, in Phoenix Park in 1882. Fenians led by O'Donovan Rossa also organized a campaign of dynamite sabotage in England in the 1880s that was the forerunner of Irish Republican Army operations in modern times. But apart from occasional acts of Fenian terror there was no significant revolutionary activity in Ireland for forty years after the 1867 rising. The Clan na Gael was somewhat more active in America, although riddled by internal conflicts, and it broadened its interests to support Parnell's constitutional nationalism and the Irish Land League in the 1880s.

Revolutionary nationalism in the Fenian tradition was revived in America by a reorganization of the Clan na Gael in 1900. In 1907 the Clan sent Tom Clarke back to Ireland. He was a convicted Fenian dynamiter who had been released in 1898 after serving fifteen years in an English prison and had emigrated to the U.S.A . His task now was to put new life into the IRB which had been slumbering for many years. In Dublin he joined a new, young leadership group which included Denis McCullough, Bulmer Hobson, Sean MacDiarmada, P. S. O'Hegarty, and others, but the organization probably numbered fewer than two thousand members and was maintained in large part by financial grants from the Clan na Gael in America. It was incapable of staging a rebellion, and its most successful policy was to infiltrate its members into leading positions in other nationalist organizations, one of which was Sinn Fein.

Sinn Fein owed its existence to Arthur Griffith, the editor of *United Irishman*, first published in 1899. Griffith used his newspaper to popularize and expand a strategy first suggested by the Young Irelanders and O'Connell, that is the systematic withdrawal of Irish representatives from Westminster and the creation, de facto, of a parallel system of Irish government and law that would deny England the power actually to govern Ireland. Griffith argued that Ireland should follow the example of Hungarian nationalists who had won independence in 1861, within the framework of the dual Austro-Hungarian monarchy, by refusing to send Hungarian members to the Austrian Imperial Parliament. In 1900 he formed an organization, Cumann na nGaedheal, to promote his views, and in 1905 he joined with another loosely organized nationalist group of IRB members, the Dungannon Clubs, to form Sinn Fein, a name drawn from the Irish word for "ourselves."

Sinn Fein was no match for the constitutional nationalist movement, and its candidate for parliament was soundly beaten in a 1908 by-election, but it did attract considerable support, reaching a peak in the period between 1908 and 1910. More important, it became, with Griffith's approval, a front for revolutionary nationalism. Indeed, the

Easter Rising was immediately christened "the Sinn Fein Rebellion" by the press and the government although Sinn Fein had played no formal role in it at all. After the Rising the organization officially became the political wing of the revolutionary movement, and it set about implementing the strategy of withdrawal from the U.K. Parliament that Griffith had outlined earlier. Sinn Fein remains today a political party and the political wing of the Irish Republican Army in Northern Ireland, and its members of Parliament still refuse to take their seats.

The IRB continued its own separate and secret existence. In 1910, for example, it launched a newspaper, *Irish Freedom*, to carry its message to the public, but it would have accomplished nothing if the situation in Ireland had not changed dramatically between 1912 and 1914. As we shall see in Chapter 6, constitutional nationalism was poised for the victory of home rule in Parliament in 1913 when the Ulster Protestants organized a paramilitary force, the Ulster Volunteers, to resist home rule by force. Members of the IRB were critically important in organizing the nationalists' reply, the Irish Volunteers. This organization was first suggested by an essentially moderate man, Eoin MacNeill, professor of early Irish history at University College, Dublin, but a third of its organizing committee was made up of members of the secret IRB. Patrick Pearse, who had joined the IRB in 1913, became the director of military operations of the Irish Volunteers that year.

The Irish Volunteers quickly grew, and in 1914 John Redmond, who saw them as a threat to the authority of the Irish Party, forced his nominees into a commanding position on the committee of the organization. What he and the chairman of the Volunteers, MacNeill, did not know was that key positions in the command structure were held by members of the IRB, those such as Patrick Pearse, Sean MacDiarmada, Bulmer Hobson, and The O'Rahilly.[18] It was they who led a small number of the Volunteers into the Easter Rising in 1916.

CONCLUSION

Had the three varieties of Irish nationalism—constitutional, romantic, and revolutionary—been combined, A. D. Smith's model of national development outlined in Chapter 3 would have been complete. It would have been a sophisticated political organization, effectively led; mobilizing enormous public support; recognizing and cultivating a distinctive national culture; and inspired to heroic deeds by the myths and legends of the past. To some degree, of course, the three movements were intertwined. The Young Irelanders and some of the leaders in 1916, Pearse above all, were both revolutionary and romantic nationalists. Fenians and Gaelic Leaguers no doubt voted for candidates of the Irish Party at general elections, and the number of people thrilled by Fenian exploits went far beyond the formal membership of the IRB. Furthermore, until Parnell's death constitutional nationalism operated with the covert support of violent people. Even in John Redmond's day, Irish members of Parliament who argued for moderation and home rule at Westminster often preached national independence and flirted with extremists when fundraising in Ireland and America.

Nevertheless, the fact remains that Irish nationalism was divided. As a movement, constitutional nationalism and the Irish party were far removed from the visceral hatreds of the Fenians, and their concerns were more pragmatic and material than those of romantic nationalism. The Irish party played no part in the cultural revival and was therefore divorced from some of the best minds in Ireland, particularly among the young, who wanted more than a home rule parliament in Dublin. As Oliver MacDonagh explains, "The orthodox Irish Nationalist of the 1880s and 1890s was scarcely aware that a 'problem' of anglicization existed."[19] Yet constitutional nationalism, shorn of the emotional power of an association with the Irish Land League, and isolated from important currents of cultural change and revolutionary agitation in Ireland, still represented by far the strongest of the three nationalist movements in 1912. It was powerful, popular, and successful. Its adherents were already well established in the Irish administration and the judiciary, and it appeared set for its final triumph, home rule. Romantic nationalism had a relatively small following of urban intellectuals and revolutionary nationalism was starved of funds and followers. But revolutions are not created by mass movements. Most of the people are spectators when the guns begin to fire. Events finally conspired to rob the constitutional nationalists of their prize and hand it to the minority, the revolutionaries in the years 1916 to 1922. In Chapters 7 and 8 we will see that the constitutionalists' progress towards home rule was halted by Protestant resistance in 1914, and this gave the revolutionaries the opportunity which they seized at Easter, 1916.

1 A. D. Smith, *National Identity* (London, 1991), p. 93.
2 Robert Kee, *The Green Flag* (New York, 1972), pp. 196–98.
3 Lawrence McCaffrey, *The Irish Question, 1800–1922* (Lexington, 1968), p. 41.
4 Dangerfield, p. 31.
5 F. S. L. Lyons, *Ireland Since the Famine* (London, 1971), pp. 219–42.
6 Foster, p. 455.
7 Lyons, p. 336.
8 Patrick Pearse, *The Best of Pearse*, Proinsias Mac Aonghusa and Liam O Réagáin, eds. (Cork, 1967), p. 134.
9 Quoted by J. J. Lee, "In search of Patrick Pearse," in *Revising the Rising*, Máirín Ní Dhonnchadha and Theo Dorgan, eds. (Derry, 1991), p.127.
10 Pearse, p. 125.
11 Malcolm Brown, *The Politics of Irish Literature* (Seattle, 1972), p. 37.
12 Brown, p. 21.
13 Thomas Flanagan, "Rebellion and Style: John Mitchel and the Jail Journal," *Irish University Review* I (Autumn 1970), pp. 4–5.
14 Kee, p. 164.
15 Ibid., p. 168.
16 Ibid., pp. 284–286; McCaffrey, p. 69.
17 Brown, p. 8.
18 "The" is an old Irish title representing the senior living descendant of a Clan chief.
19 MacDonagh, *Ireland*, p. 64.

CHAPTER 6

America and the Irish Problem

THE PROCLAMATION OF THE IRISH REPUBLIC IN 1916 spoke of Ireland being "supported by her exiled children in America," which indicates that there was, indeed still is, an American dimension to the Irish problem. If we are to understand the Easter Rising, we have to know something about Irish-Americans. They were the ones who financed and sustained Irish nationalism, both constitutional and revolutionary, in the years before the Rising, and they were the ones who kept alive the dream of an independent Ireland when most at home would have settled for less.

THE IRISH AMERICANS

The first Irish emigration to America was from both Irish communities in the eighteenth century, but a particularly large group traveled from the Protestant north, including Presbyterians. British policies in Ireland in the eighteenth century discriminated against Presbyterians as well as Catholics, and many of them emigrated for religious freedom and greater economic opportunities in America where they became known as Scots-Irish, meaning the Ulster Presbyterian descendants of seventeenth-century Scottish settlers. There were only thirty thousand or so Catholics in the American colonies in 1789, and in 1801 it was still possible for George Washington to tell the largely Protestant American people in his Farewell Address, "With slight shades of difference you have the same religion, manners, habits and political principles." By the mid-nineteenth century, however, the composition of the population had begun to change as immigrants from a variety of countries found in America a haven from political, religious, and economic distress. The first great wave of non-British immigrants was made up of Irish Catholics who had begun to leave Ireland before the famine but whose emigration turned into a torrent after 1845. Within a few years they had made the Irish question almost as much an issue in American politics as it was in British politics.

Many of the prefamine Irish immigrants were skilled artisans, tenant farmers, and others who were not wretchedly poor, but then came the famine. Between 1845 and 1854 1.5 million Irish emigrated to the United States. Many of these were famine poor whom McCaffrey calls "refugees from disaster."[1] Huge numbers of them arrived destitute, becoming inhabitants of urban, ethnic ghettos in the east. Their lives were grim because ghetto problems of the past were similar to those of today. Later in the century, from 1870 or so, Irish immigrants began to mirror improved living conditions in Ireland so that, taken as a whole, they proved to be a diverse group of people. The 1910 United States Census identified 4.5 million residents who had been born in Ireland or were the children of at least one Irish-born parent. Millions more were second- or third-generation Americans who considered themselves Irish. They provided hard labor for American industries and railroads, but some achieved economic and social prominence. By the turn of the century they could be counted among the most successful people in America: railroad barons, a justice of the New York Supreme Court, governors, and congressmen. They were also supremely successful machine politicians, controlling major cities such as Boston and New York. Not the least of their accomplishments was that they supported a rich and powerful Catholic Church and a large system of Catholic schools and colleges.

Irish-American Catholics remained resolutely Irish, whereas Irish-American Protestants were quickly assimilated into the predominantly Anglo culture of the U.S.A. Perhaps seventeen American presidents could claim Irish ancestry, but only the one Catholic, John F. Kennedy, is popularly thought of as Irish. In an important sense, Irish Catholics were forced to remain Irish. They were the victims of nineteenth-century American nativism, an anti-Catholic, anti-immigrant hatred which mirrored English nativism of the same period. In both America and England, Irish Catholics were disparaged in print and cartoon as drunkards, layabouts, thieves, and apes. The Know-Nothing party of the 1850s was anti-Irish, as were the American Protective Association and the populism of the 1880s and 1890s. The Irish were therefore forced to turn to each other for support. They joined a host of Irish social, political, sporting, and benevolent societies. In addition, in the absence of the welfare state, the ghetto Irish were organized into potent voting blocs by machine Democratic politicians who discovered that by providing jobs and relief for the poor they could control the Irish vote. Finally, at the very heart, or perhaps soul, of the Irish-American community lay the Roman Catholic Church.

As a result of these social forces and affiliations, few Catholic Irish Americans were able, and few would have chosen, to live outside the Irish community. They lived and worshiped and played together, and they remembered together, even if their memories were generations old and distorted. What they remembered was England's cruel repression that had driven them out of Ireland. As Kirby Miller reminds us, the Irish were both immigrants and exiles, with strong resentments from having been forced from their homes.[2] In 1869, an Irish-American author, D. P. Conyngham, issued a very solemn warning to England when he asked, "How is it that the Government of England is so blind to the ruin that a people so numerous and powerful in foreign countries, and hating her so intensely, is sure to bring on her in her hour of troubles? It might be politic to try conciliation, instead of coercion, on such a people."[3]

As Conyngham predicted, Irish Americans did work to ruin England. They sought to influence American foreign policy against England, they supported the constitutional movement for home rule in Ireland, and they supported the revolutionary movement in Ireland that led to Easter Week, 1916, a rebellion that certainly came during England's hour of troubles.

IRISH AMERICANS AND AMERICAN FOREIGN POLICY

The Irish in America and the Irish in Ireland had quite different attitudes towards Britain, and the key to this difference lay in the phenomenon that one can call Irish-American nationalism. By 1900 a majority of Irish Americans had either been born in America or had left Ireland many years before. The Ireland most of them knew from experience or from tales told by parents and grandparents was impoverished and enslaved. They knew little of land reforms or the social and economic progress of the postfamine years. Perhaps more than the Irish who had remained behind, therefore, Irish Americans passionately desired Ireland's liberation from English tyranny.

Thomas Brown has also shown that a specifically American form of Irish nationalism flourished as a response to the plight of the Ireland the immigrants had fled and the problems of economic hardship and nativist rejection that they encountered in America.[4] Irish Americans attributed their rejection in America to the impoverished and enslaved condition of the Ireland they had left. They reacted by seeking self-respect by working to liberate their homeland, and seeking acceptance in their adopted land by demonstrating a fierce loyalty to America. They expressed their patriotism in a fiercely anglophobic Americanism which managed to combine the interests of America with the interests of Ireland. They thought of England as both the oppressor of Ireland and the traditional enemy of American democracy. As a result it was more natural for the Irish in America to plot the downfall of England than it was for the Irish in Ireland. McCaffrey writes, "Irish nationalism jelled and flourished in the ghettos of urban America as a search for identity, an expression of vengeance, and a quest for respectability."[5]

It was this American component in Irish Nationalism that explains the determination of many Irish Americans to work not only for Ireland's freedom but for Britain's downfall, something few were planning in Ireland. For example, John Mitchel, the Young Irelander who was rescued from an Australian convict settlement by an Irish-American expedition and brought to America in 1853, pleaded Russia's case against Britain in his newspaper, *The Citizen*, during the Crimean War; and the Irish-American press supported Russia against England's ally, Japan, during the Russo-Japanese War of 1904–1905. During the Boer War in 1899 and 1900, Irish Americans led a powerful anti-British agitation with mass meetings throughout America, and they were largely responsible for the anti-British statements included in both the Democratic and Republican Party platforms in the presidential election year of 1900. An Irish-American ambulance corps was sent to South Africa, where its members abandoned medicine and took up arms with the Boers. In addition, in 1897, 1904, and 1912, American arbitration treaties with Britain were denounced by Irish Americans as alliances and were defeated in the U.S. Senate. Indeed, the Irish maintained a continuous attack on anything that might have suggested Anglo-American friendship, and in 1907 German and Irish-American organizations began to work together in anticipation of a future European war.

In the years before World War I, Irish Americans acted as a critically important element in a number of coalitions: with anti-imperialist Democrats, with senators determined to protect their foreign relations prerogatives against open-ended arbitration treaties, with German Americans, Russians, Boers, and even Indian nationalists from South Asia, at various times. In every case the Irish-American interest was the same, to damage Britain. It was natural, therefore, that when World War I began, some Irish Americans supported the German cause and almost all the rest demanded that the United States maintain neutrality. As the historian T. A. Bailey wrote,

> From the outset it was clear that the American people would find it more than ordinarily difficult to avoid taking sides. This was a world war; and the United States, the historic asylum of the oppressed, contained a "'menagerie of nationalists.'"[6]

German and Irish Americans, for example, were just two of the communities that took sides in the European war, and in October 1914, President Wilson confessed to the U.S. ambassador to England,

> More and more, from day to day, the elements (I mean the several racial elements) of our population seem to grow restless and catch more and more the fever of the contest. We are trying to keep all possible spaces cool, and the only means by which we can do so is to make it demonstrably clear that we

are doing everything that it is possible to do to define and defend neutral rights.[7]

During the war, and particularly after the United States entered it in April 1917, President Wilson sent appeal after appeal to the United Kingdom government asking it to resolve the Irish question for the sake of Anglo-American harmony and the war effort.

IRISH AMERICANS AND CONSTITUTIONAL NATIONALISM

Irish American nationalism had an important effect on American politics and foreign policy, but it had an equally important impact on politics in the United Kingdom. After Parnell became leader of the Irish party in 1880 he turned to America for financial support. At first, American funds went to fight the Land War, but after the Irish Land Act of 1881 money was available to support Irish members of Parliament. Between 1880 and 1914 an almost continuous stream of Irish politicians visited the United States, as well as Australia and Canada, to raise funds for the Irish party. Members of Parliament received no salaries until 1911, when annual payments of £400 were first made, but before this date Irish members who needed financial help received it largely from American sources. F. S. L. Lyons estimates that 50 percent of the eighty or more Irish members received aid in the years 1900 to 1910 and that £70,000 ($350,000) was raised.[8] Contemporary accounts suggest that this estimate may be too low. Parnell himself went to America in 1880 and addressed a joint session of Congress, so important had the Irish question already become there. He returned with £20,000.

John Redmond made an American tour in 1883, when he collected £15,000, and toured again in 1886, 1895, and 1899. He returned from this last tour convinced that the split in the Irish party caused by the Parnell divorce scandal in 1890 had seriously impaired the American fundraising effort. The reunion of the party under his leadership in 1900 was brought about in part because of this diagnosis. Thereafter, Redmond and other leaders, such as Joseph Devlin, John Dillon, William Redmond, and T. P. O'Connor, returned regularly to gather funds in the United States and Canada. O'Connor visited America six times in all. In 1901 John Redmond formed the United Irish League of America which became an enormously successful auxiliary of the Irish party. It sponsored large meetings in dozens of cities, and its activities were widely reported in the press. It also raised very large sums of money for election and parliamentary expenses.

The success of Redmond's constitutional agitation in America was a damaging blow to those Irish Americans who favored a revolution in Ireland. However, the conclusion that the Irish in America found it easier to work for England's downfall than did the Irish in Ireland was clearly demonstrated in 1914. In August of that year, as war broke out in Europe, John Redmond stood in the House of Commons to pledge Ireland's support to England in the war against Germany. Almost immediately the United Irish League collapsed in America, and Redmond's leadership was rejected by the American Irish. An interesting aspect of Redmond's campaign in America had been that the same crowds which came to cheer him could also be mobilized by the Clan na Gael to oppose England whenever Anglo-American relations appeared in danger of becoming too harmonious. With the collapse of the United Irish League, the Clan monopolized the leadership of Irish America.

IRISH AMERICANS AND REVOLUTIONARY NATIONALISM

We have already seen in Chapter 5 that there were very few active revolutionaries in Ireland in the twenty or thirty years before 1916. In large part this was due to the general improvements in Irish life and the political success of the home rule movement. The relative calm also reflected the fact that England had driven several generations of revolutionaries out of Ireland, most of them to the United States. Indeed, a nineteenth-century commentator wrote, "The result of the abortive insurrection of 1848 was to change the base of Irish revolution from Ireland to America."[9]

One such revolutionary was Tom Clarke, who was to be executed for his part in the Easter Rising. He first went to America in 1881 but was captured in England in 1883 on a Clan na Gael sabotage mission. He was imprisoned until 1898 and left again for America. By 1907 he was back in Dublin with Clan na Gael funds to reorganize the Irish

Republican Brotherhood. He and all the others had used America as John Mitchel had declared he would use it when he arrived in 1853: "I mean to make use of the freedom guaranteed to me as a citizen . . . of America to help and stimulate the movement of European Democracy and especially of Irish independence."[10]

Irish revolutionaries in America supplied funds for the secret IRB and formed its American partner, the Fenian Brotherhood. By 1865 the brotherhood numbered fifty thousand, and British prisons were very soon loaded with Irish Americans arrested for treason or sedition when they returned to Ireland or England. Many participated in the Fenian rising of 1867 in Ireland and Fenian attacks on Canada discussed above in Chapter 5.

The Fenian Brotherhood collapsed in the early 1870s, but another Irish-American revolutionary organization, the Clan na Gael, founded in 1867, and led by John Devoy after his arrival in 1871, survived to carry the revolutionary cause into the twentieth century. The Clan supported Parnell and the Land League agitation, but it never lost sight of revolution. For example, it waged a campaign of bombing in England from 1883 to 1885 that closely paralleled recent IRA terrorism. The Clan suffered from debilitating internal conflicts in the 1880s and 1890s, but it was revived in 1900 by John Devoy and Judge Daniel Cohalan, an American-born lawyer who was also a New York machine politician. Its members were still pledged to use physical force to liberate Ireland, but it committed no violent acts in the years before World War I. British diplomats frequently saw Clan dynamiters in their dreams, but the organization actually concentrated on organizing the anti-English activities described earlier in this chapter, opposition to arbitration treaties and the Boer War, and cooperation with German Americans in preparation for World War I, for example. Ireland was not ready for revolution as even the most dedicated Irish-American revolutionary could see. John Devoy was later to write, "From 1871 to 1916 [the IRB] was maintained almost entirely by the moral and material support from the Clan na Gael. Envoys from the IRB attended every Convention of the Clan na Gael and went back to carry on the work."[11]

Times were bad for revolutionaries, but the Clan leaders bided their time and did what they could in Ireland. For example, they supported Sinn Fein in its infancy because it opposed Redmond's Irish party. The Clan regarded constitutional nationalism as a threat to eventual Irish independence and did anything it could to weaken its effects. The Clan's most important revolutionary act in the years before World War I was to send Tom Clarke to Dublin in 1907 to reorganize the almost extinct IRB. From the cover of his tobacconist shop, Clarke waited and planned for Ireland's opportunity. In New York, John Devoy also waited. He had never forgotten something he wrote in 1881:

> If Ireland wins her freedom, she must wade to it through blood and suffering and sacrifice. . . . The people at home must be prepared—they must be armed. . . . We in America must do more than make speeches and subscribe money to keep the agitator alive! An agitation that must be fed and fostered and subsidized from abroad has nothing in it. Let us devote some of our spare cash to preparing Ireland for the final ordeal.[12]

CONCLUSION

The American connection was critically important for Irish nationalism. For example, it provided financial support that brought constitutional nationalism and home rule to the brink of victory in 1914. Furthermore, British politicians were well aware that Anglo-American relations would continue to suffer if the Irish question remained unresolved. For our purpose, however, the most significant American contribution was the revolutionary one. As Devoy made clear, the Irish in America worked steadily to prepare Ireland for the final ordeal. Revolutionary nationalism was terribly weak in Ireland in 1914, but it was being kept alive by Irish-American money, and its moment was approaching.

1 Lawrence McCaffrey, *The Irish Diaspora in America* (Bloomington, IN, 1976), Chap. 4.
2 Miller, passim.
3 D. P. Conyngham, *The Irish Brigade and its Campaigns* (Boston, 1869), p. 81.
4 Thomas N. Brown, *Irish-American Nationalism, 1870–1890* (Philadelphia, 1966).
5 McCaffrey, p. 107.
6 Thomas A. Bailey, *A Diplomatic History of the American People* (New York, 1950), p. 610.

7 Alan J. Ward, *Ireland and Anglo-American Relations, 1899–1921* (London, 1969), p. 85.

8 F. S. L. Lyons, *The Irish Parliamentary Party, 1890–1910* (London, 1951), Chap. 6.

9 Philip H. Bagenal, *The American-Irish and their Influence on Irish Politics* (London, 1882), p. 111.

10 Florence Gibson, *The Attitudes of the New York Irish Towards State and National Affairs, 1848–1892* (New York, 1951), p. 65.

11 John Devoy, *Recollections of a Rebel* (New York, 1929), p. 392.

12 Bagenal, p. 223.

CHAPTER 7

Three Home Rule Bills and the Rise of Unionism

WE HAVE ALREADY NOTED IN CHAPTER 4 THAT, IN AN organizational sense, constitutional nationalism was the most successful of the forms of Catholic nationalism in Ireland. Its success can be measured by the fact that three bills for Irish self-government, known popularly as home rule bills, were introduced by the Liberal governments of Prime Minister William Gladstone, in 1886 and 1893, and Herbert Asquith in 1912. Each of these governments depended on the votes of the Irish Party for its majority in the House of Commons. In the December 1910 election, for example, the Liberals and Conservatives were actually tied, at 272 seats each. The new Labour Party had forty-two seats but the Irish Party, with eighty-four seats, held the balance. The price for its support was home rule. However, the success of constitutional nationalism, which seemed to be moving inexorably towards Irish self-government, provoked a counternationalism in Ireland, the nationalism of Irish Protestants, better known as Irish unionism. The clash between the two would deny the constitutionalists their victory and open the door to revolution in 1916. In this chapter we will consider the relationship between the home rule bills and unionism.

The 1886 home rule bill was defeated by 341 votes to 311 in the House of Commons because ninety-three Liberals deserted the government to vote with the Conservative opposition. Had it passed the House of Commons it would certainly have lost in the House of Lords. Indeed, when the 1893 bill was approved by the Commons by

347 votes to 267, it was absolutely crushed by the Lords, by 419 votes to 41. Circumstances had changed radically by the time of the introduction of the third home rule bill in 1912. This was because of the passage of the 1911 Parliament Act, which deprived the peers of their veto. Henceforward, the House of Lords could only delay legislation for two years. If a bill were to pass through the House of Commons three times, in successive sessions and identical language, it would move on for the royal assent over the opposition of the Lords. This meant, of course, that the third home rule bill, which was introduced into the Commons in 1912, would have become law after its third passage through the House of Commons in 1914 had the Ulster unionists and their colleagues in the British Conservative party not threatened civil war in Ireland to stop it.

This sense that the Irish were robbed in 1914 has led historians to concentrate on the act of "robbery" rather than on what was stolen. The question of whether the home rule bills were good or bad has been neglected, no doubt because the constitutional issues involved were very complex. We ought to ask, however, if the bills were really capable of finally settling the Irish problem, as Parnell and his successors insisted they were.

HOME RULE AND THE CONSTITUTION[1]

Home rule was a form of what is now known in the United Kingdom as "devolution," which is the process of creating subordinate regional parliaments to handle regional affairs, each drawing its authority from legislation passed in the United Kingdom Parliament. Broadly speaking, regional parliaments deal with purely regional matters and the Parliament in London deals with two matters. It has responsibility for matters of concern to the whole United Kingdom, such as defense, foreign relations, the monarchy, trade, national economic policy, and so on. Then too, it has responsibility for regions which do not have their own parliaments. The devolution that the U.K. government introduced in 1998 created regional parliaments in Northern Ireland, Scotland, and Wales, but England still lacks a legislature of its own and is governed by the U.K. Parliament. The home rule bills introduced in 1886, 1893, and 1912 were different in that they would have created only one regional parliament, in Ireland, leaving the affairs of the other regions and the affairs of the United Kingdom as a whole to be handled by the U.K. Parliament in London.

The three Irish home rule bills were nearly identical in their essential aspects. They proposed that a parliament be established in Dublin for Irish affairs. Ireland would have its own government, with ministers drawn from this parliament, and almost all of its domestic life would be in Irish hands, with the exception that the London Parliament would retain most revenue raising powers, and no law could be passed to endow, establish, or restrict religion. The United Kingdom Parliament would continue to legislate for the U.K. as a whole and for the regions without parliaments.

No legislation of this kind could perfectly satisfy everyone but all these home rule bills had defects that would have made them very difficult to operate successfully. We should consider, very briefly, three particular flaws; the principle of representation, the constitutional relationship between the parliaments in Dublin and Westminster, and financial relations.

The Representation Dilemma

A representation dilemma arose in home rule because of the two roles assigned to the U.K. Parliament in London. As we have seen, it had the job of legislating for both the United Kingdom and the regions which had no parliaments of their own. This meant that the Irish members of Parliament in London would have had the right to participate not only in United Kingdom affairs, which was reasonable because Ireland was still in the union, but in English, Scottish and Welsh affairs too, because these were still handled by the U.K. Parliament.

This problem led Gladstone to propose in 1886 that the Irish should not sit in London because it would be unfair for them to participate in British affairs while having a parliament of their own. But excluding them meant that they would have no say at all in United Kingdom matters which affected them, which was surely unfair. Gladstone changed his mind in 1893 and agreed that the Irish could sit in London, but this simply reversed the problem. Now Irish M.P.s could vote on United Kingdom matters, which was fair, and on British matters, which was not. Furthermore, the Irish might have an important role in deciding which party would form the government. If the selection of the government were to depend on the support of Irish M.P.s, as it did every time home rule was introduced between 1886 and 1912, then the eighty or more Irish members would actually decide which party would form the government of both the United Kingdom and Britain.

This was a dilemma for which there could be no satisfactory solution within the framework of Irish home rule. If the Irish sat in London they would be able to intervene in British affairs, but if they were excluded they would be deprived of the right to participate in United Kingdom affairs. In 1912 Asquith offered an inelegant compromise which simply pushed the problem aside. Ireland's representation in the House of Commons would be cut from eighty-five to forty-two, giving them less representation for U.K. affairs than their numbers would have justified, but far more representation for British affairs than they should have had.

The representation dilemma could have been resolved by a comprehensive reform that would have given home rule to England, Scotland, and Wales, leaving the U.K. Parliament with no regional responsibilities at all. However, Parliament was divided on the merits of the scheme, and there was no general demand for regional parliaments outside Ireland. In the absence of broad support, "home rule all round," as it was called, was considered too heavy a price to pay to appease Irish nationalists.

The Constitutional Relationship

The representation issue aside, home rule also posed other constitutional problems. The most important of these was the vagueness of the proposed relationship between the two countries. In each bill, the United Kingdom Parliament retained its legal supremacy. It could override the Dublin legislature, or even abolish home rule itself, by a simple act of Parliament. This meant that Ireland would always be at the mercy of the government in London. Furthermore, through its "advice to the Crown," which is constitutional language for the fact that the monarch must do what a government advises, the royal veto could be used by the United Kingdom government to block Irish legislation when it was sent to the monarch for the royal assent.

The point at which the United Kingdom might intervene in Irish affairs was never made clear in legislation or debate. The Liberals argued that Ireland would be protected by a "convention"—an unwritten constitutional rule—that intervention would only occur in some unspecified dire emergency, but Conservatives and Irish unionists could not imagine that a Liberal government, particularly one dependent on Irish nationalist votes in the U.K. Parliament, would ever have the courage to overrule the Irish Parliament. If that argument failed to persuade, the opponents of home rule had another that came from quite the opposite direction. They argued that if a United Kingdom government were to intervene too much in Irish affairs, it would provoke the Irish into demanding full independence. So, as these arguments ran, home rule could not win. British nonintervention in Ireland would facilitate Irish secession, and intervention would positively encourage it.

The key to the deep Conservative and unionist opposition to home rule was the belief that although the ultimate sovereignty of the U.K. Parliament was written into home rule, the Irish Parliament would surely be used as a stepping stone to independence, one way or another. But it has to be recognized that the home rule bills, as drafted, played into the hands of the opponents by being constitutionally vague on the critical issue of the proposed relationship between Ireland and the United Kingdom. In practice, good relations between the two countries would have to depend on goodwill and trust, qualities notably lacking in the history of Anglo-Irish relations.

The Financial Relationship

Many critics of home rule believed that a constitutional crisis between Britain and Ireland would arise from an invasion of Protestant religious rights by a Catholic-dominated parliament in Dublin. However, religious freedom was guaranteed in all the home rule bills and the more probable source of conflict would have been the proposed financial relationship between Ireland and the United Kingdom. The home rule bills all gave the Irish Parliament responsibility for Irish domestic programs but left control of all important taxes with the United Kingdom. There was always to be a distinction, then, between the Parliament raising money for Irish affairs in London and the Irish Parliament spending this income in Dublin. In effect, Irish domestic programs would always be framed by taxing policies set in London. In this regard, it was extremely ominous for the future of home rule that the Irish party always believed the financial terms of home rule would have to be renegotiated. John Redmond, for example, accepted the third home rule bill as a "final settlement" but added, "Admittedly it is a provisional settlement. . . . When the time for revision does come . . . we will be entitled to complete power for Ireland over the whole of our financial system."[2]

The opponents of home rule attacked these three constitutional flaws in every one of the many debates on home rule over a period of nearly thirty years. Their major concern was not to improve the legislation, because they wanted to kill home rule one way or another. If they failed to convince using one argument they would change their ground and try others. However, this political opportunism does not mean that all the criticisms were unsound. The home rule bills were not particularly good pieces of legislation.

In purely constitutional terms, the simplest remedy for the constitutional problems of home rule would have been for Britain to abandon the union and give Ireland its independence. This would have avoided the anomalies inherent in a home rule package that did not include the other regions of the United Kingdom. But such a solution was impossible. In the nineteenth century every member of the House of Commons who was not an Irish nationalist believed that an Irish settlement had to satisfy three conditions. It had to protect the union. Ireland could not be allowed to secede because that would expose the Protestant minority and British land holdings to a Catholic parliament and would set an unacceptable precedent for the colonies of the British Empire. Next, with regard to the troubled religious history of Ireland, a settlement had to protect the religious rights of the Protestant minority. Finally, a settlement had to recognize the constitutional supremacy of the United Kingdom so that the United Kingdom could overrule the Irish parliament, or even abolish it, if this were thought necessary in London.

Both of the major parties in Britain, the Liberals and Conservatives, agreed on these three conditions, so it was only by using this framework that Irish nationalism could hope to win any support in

Britain for a negotiated settlement, as Parnell well knew. Gladstone and Asquith believed that their home rule bills satisfied the three conditions, but a majority of Conservatives were always convinced that they were wrong.

PROTESTANT "NATIONALISM":
THE UNIONIST RESPONSE TO HOME RULE

It was the first home rule bill, in 1886, that led to the creation of the unionist alliance that was to deny constitutional nationalism its victory in 1914 and open the door to the Rising in 1916. The alliance included the predominantly Anglican Irish landlord class who believed that an Irish parliament would rob them of their property through expropriation or disadvantageous land reform. It included the Protestants of Ulster, predominantly Presbyterians, many of whom believed that a parliament in Dublin, dominated by Catholics, would be controlled from Rome. The Ulster Protestants included all social classes in the north, particularly the urban working class, which had frequently participated in religious riots in Belfast and other northern Irish cities. The unionist alliance also included the Orange Society, whose many lodges provided the grass-roots organization for Irish unionism in the north. Its membership grew substantially from the mid-1880s. The unionist alliance also included many allies in Britain. Most of these were Conservatives, often in Parliament and the army, who had certain interests to protect. Many owned land in Ireland. Most were determined to protect the Anglican Church of Ireland. And virtually all of them believed that Irish home rule would be the first step in the disintegration of the British Empire. As Ireland went, they argued, so would go Egypt, India, South Africa, and the rest. Finally, the unionist alliance included ninety-three Liberal M.P.s, led by Joseph Chamberlain, who defected from the Liberal Party on the 1886 home rule bill vote and became "Liberal unionists." Their votes were responsible for the defeat of the bill, by 341 votes to 311, and they did not return to the Liberal fold.

As was suggested above, the name "unionist" concealed some important distinctions. For example, there was a considerable difference between southern and northern Irish unionists. The former were distinguished by their Anglicanism, their ownership of land, and their status as an élite. They were a small minority of less than 10 percent in a population of Catholics. The northern, or Ulster, unionists had many characteristics of an ethnie. They were Protestants, including Anglicans, Presbyterians, and a small number of Methodists, and they represented every kind of occupation and social class in the north. They formed about half the population in the nine counties of traditional Ulster and about two-thirds in the six counties finally identified as Northern Ireland in the partition of 1921. The solid core of the unionists' resistance to home rule naturally lay in the northeast, the area of greatest Protestant settlement in the seventeenth century. As Patrick Buckland noted of this group, "Ulster Protestants felt that they had little in common with either the Catholic majority or the scattered and largely landed Protestant minority in the agricultural South. This feeling created the Ulster question and Ulster unionism." As unionism developed there was no dialogue with nationalists, only, as Buckland describes it, "mutual recrimination in slanging matches undertaken with a view to influencing opinion in Great Britain."[3]

In one important sense, Ulster unionism was unlike Catholic nationalism, and the difference makes it a little difficult to identify the two as equivalent nationalisms. Unionists could be said to have had two collective identities, not one. On the one hand they claimed to be British, and the name "Ulster loyalist," or just "loyalist," is often used to describe this identity. Many unionist symbols and values relate to this identity, particularly extreme loyalty to the Crown. This mutes the sense that unionism is a distinctive ethnic identity. Apart from a very few people on the political fringe, unionists have never sought independence, or even regional political autonomy until it was given to them in 1921. On the other hand, unionists were very much the unionists of Ulster, with their own Irish history, symbols, heroes, myths, attitudes, and values that set them apart from Britain.

Unionism's core Ulster characteristic was a dour, Reformation Protestantism, particularly in the Presbyterian community, the largest in the north, which could no more mix with Irish Catholicism than oil with water. Each was suspiciously exclusive of the other. Unionism's most important Irish auxiliary was the Loyal Orange Order, a kind of masonic order named after William of Orange which was organized in 1795, after Catholics and Protestants had clashed in Armagh, Northern Ireland. In the nineteenth century it established a tradition of triumphalist parades to celebrate a very Protestant interpretation of Irish history, although historian Brian Walker points out that the bulk of the Protestant population did not identify with these celebrations until the 1880s.[4]

Unionism developed as a political ideology in response to the growth of Catholic nationalism, and with a particular fierceness because by the 1880s the Protestants of Ireland were rapidly becoming a people under siege. As Irish nationalism gained in strength, so too did unionism. Gladstone could insist that home rule posed no threat to the Protestant community because the Dublin parliament would be constitutionally subordinate to Westminster, but the unionists simply did not believe him. What was at stake, they believed, was the future of the union with Britain, which they believed was a solemn compact intended to preserve their land, religion, and status. Catholic emancipation, the disestablishment of the Anglican Church of Ireland, the enlargement of the franchise to benefit Catholics, and land reform were seen as cumulatively eroding the Protestants' position in Ireland, and this made them more determined than ever to cling to what was left, which was the union itself. Unionism was also at its strongest in the heartland of the Irish industrial economy. Belfast was the major industrial city in Ireland, which many in the north took to be a sign of the progress of, indeed the inherent superiority of, northern Protestant stock.

Improvements in communications and education and the growth of the popular press affected unionism in the same way in the northeast of Ireland that it affected nationalism in the south and west. Unionism had its political, religious, and cultural leaders who crafted a distinctive unionist world view in the later part of the nineteenth century which very much served their interests, particularly Protestant church leaders who wanted no part of a "Catholic parliament" in Dublin, and the industrialists and capitalists of the north who flourished in the United Kingdom and saw no future for themselves in a self-governing Ireland dominated by rural interests. Unionism had its own organic intelligentsia of clergy, teachers, lodge officers, and middle class professionals, particularly in Belfast, to spread the message. Unionism also had at its disposal the most developed provincial press of any part of Ireland.

As the Liberal party in Ireland was destroyed by Parnell's Irish party in the 1880s, so too was the Conservative party in Ireland replaced by Ulster unionism, but Conservative politicians in Britain shared the Irish Protestants' antipathy to home rule and learned to co-opt it as a party political weapon against Liberal governments. To restore Conservative fortunes, Lord Randolph Churchill advised in 1885, "the Orange card" should be played. He added later, "Ulster will fight and Ulster will be right."[5] The words "Conservative" and "unionist" quickly became synonymous, and in 1912, the British Conservative party changed its name to the Conservative and Unionist party in recognition of the importance of the Ulster question in British politics.

The unionist alliance succeeded in defeating the 1886 Home Rule Bill in the House of Commons, and the 1893 bill was defeated in the House of Lords. Indeed, it was clear that the very large Conservative majority in the Lords would vote against home rule indefinitely. But then, the Liberals changed the rules by destroying the Lords' veto in 1911, as mentioned above.

In 1909, the House of Lords provoked a constitutional crisis by rejecting the Liberals' budget, which contained a number of social reforms. Two elections were subsequently fought on the issue of the power of the Lords, in January and December 1910, and both produced Liberal governments led by Herbert Asquith that were once again dependent on Irish Party support. Two pieces of legislation consequently followed, reform of the House of Lords and the third Irish home rule bill. Legislation could now only be delayed by the Lords for a period of about two years, not defeated. When the government introduced the third home rule bill in April 1912, it was thought that it would become law in 1914.

In 1912, however, unionists believed that the case for home rule had grown weaker, not stronger, since 1886. They noted, for example, that the Conservative governments of Lord Salisbury (1895–1902) and Arthur Balfour (1902–1905), and the Liberal governments of Sir Henry Campbell-Bannerman (1905–1908) and Herbert Asquith (1908–1916), had introduced a number of reforms which had resolved many of Ireland's material grievances. These included local government reform in 1898, the creation of the Department of Agriculture and Technical Instruction for Ireland in 1899, and establishment of a Catholic University in 1908. The most important measure was the Land Act of 1903 which ultimately enabled two hundred thousand Irish tenant farmers to buy the land they farmed on favorable terms. The unionists, measuring Ireland's problems materially, believed that an Irish parliament was even less necessary than before, and they found it hard to understand why constitutional nationalism would not disappear.

The arguments already used against home rule in 1886 and 1893 took on a new urgency in 1912. The constitutional weaknesses and dangers inherent in home rule were identified yet again, and the Irish party was accused of being separatist in disguise, using home rule as a step towards full independence. Unionists even used John Redmond's own words to condemn him. In the United States in 1910, he had said, "[Home rule] concessions are only valuable because they strengthen the arms of the Irish people to push on to the great goal of independence."[6] Redmond tried to counter by insisting, "We want peace with [England] and we deny we are separatists. We say we are willing, as Parnell was willing, to accept a subordinate Parliament created by statute of this Imperial Legislature as a final settlement of Ireland's claim."[7] But unionists simply did not believe him.

Even if it was true that Irish nationalists would accept home rule as final, as Redmond claimed, unionists still had an impressive argument remaining in their repertoire. Ireland, they argued, was not a single nation, as the nationalists insisted, but two. If the nationalists of Ireland were entitled to self-determination, then so too were the unionists. Joseph Chamberlain had made this point in the House of Commons in 1886, to a chorus of Irish nationalists' denials, and it was often repeated in 1912. By then, of course, Catholic nationalism had become even less acceptable to the unionists than before because it had come to be defined by romantic nationalists as exclusively Gaelic. The unionists certainly did not believe they belonged to that kind of Irish nation.

The Irish party tried hard to counter the two-nation argument. John Redmond, for example, insisted, "The two-nation theory is to us an abomination and a blasphemy."[8] Ireland, he argued, was one nation, not two. But although the two-nation theory was not well articulated in the debates on home rule, it was fundamental to the unionist position, and one of the important effects of the crisis in Northern Ireland since the 1960s had been the belated recognition, in both Northern Ireland and the Irish Republic, that Ireland does contain two nations, or at least two quite distinct political and cultural communities, which can only be brought together gradually, and by mutual consent.

CONCLUSION

There probably existed a unionist ethnic community in Northern Ireland, although its own definition of itself as simultaneously Irish and British blurred its image. It certainly knew what it was not. It was not Catholic or Gaelic, and the various forms of Catholic nationalism it confronted, constitutional, romantic, and revolutionary, were alienating and unappealing. But the unionist identity was not really British either. Its most powerful historical memories were different from Britain's because they were set in Ireland not the mainland, and unionists also had a sense that they were a colonial outpost under siege. They had a strong sense that time and options were running out for them unless they took decisive control of the situation. They were like the whites of the British colony of Rhodesia, who declared themselves to be an independent state under white rule in 1964. Or one can find similarities in South Africa, where whites turned to apartheid in 1948 to protect their identity and status. In each case a community of settlers felt threatened by indigenous people more numerous than they who claimed the same the territory.

Nationalism grows out of community identity, but it has to be triggered and led. In Northern Ireland the most important triggering mechanism for unionism was the growth of Catholic nationalism and the growing sense in Northern Ireland that unless Protestants took control of their own destiny, they would be sacrificed by Britain. In the next chapter we will consider the form that their resistence took in the years before World War I.

1 For a detailed discussion of the constitutional aspects of Irish home rule, see Alan J. Ward, *The Irish Constitutional Tradition: Responsible Government and Modern Ireland* (Washington, DC, 1994), pp. 50–100.

2 R. J. Lawrence, *The Government of Northern Ireland: Public Finance and Public Services, 1921–1964* (Oxford, 1965), p. 189.

3 Patrick Buckland, *Irish Unionism Two: Ulster Unionism and the Origins of Northern Ireland, 1886–1922* (Dublin, 1973), p. xxix, xxxv.

4 Brian Walker, *Dancing to History's Tune: History, Myth, and Politics in Ireland* (Belfast, 1996), p. 5.

5 Robert Kee, *The Green Flag*, pp. 400–401.

6 Ian Malcolm, "Home Rule All Round," *Nineteenth Century*, v. 68, Nov. 1910, pp. 791–799.

7 London *Times*, 12 April 1912, p. 14.

8 Denis R. Gwynn, *The History of Partition, 1912–1925* (Dublin, 1950), p. 64.

CHAPTER 8

The Constitutional Crisis of 1912–1914: Preparing for Rebellion

FROM THE PERSPECTIVE OF THE MODERN IRISH Republic, it would be natural to see the Easter Rising as the turning point in modern Irish history. It was, after all, the act that was to lead directly to the new Irish state six years later. But from the broader perspective of Anglo-Irish relations, the turning point may have already occurred two years earlier when the constitutional nationalists had a great victory snatched from their grasp. The third home rule bill was about to become law in 1914 when it was blocked by the unionists of Ulster using the threat of civil war. The Irish party had played by the rules of the parliamentary game only to find that its opponents had not. World War I delayed the reckoning and provided a respite from the greatest constitutional crisis in the United Kingdom since the overthrow of James II in 1688, but it was a respite from which the constitutionalists never recovered.

An appreciation of the Easter Rising, then, has to include an appreciation of the events of 1912 to 1914. Was there a genuine opportunity then to settle the Irish problem with home rule that was missed? Or was this simply a way station to the inevitable victory of revolutionary nationalism in 1916, the real turning point in modern history? In this chapter we will explore these questions.

ULSTER PREPARES TO REBEL

The arguments for and against home rule had changed little since 1886 and 1893, but in 1912, with the introduction of the third home rule bill, the Unionists changed their tactics. Their dissent became rebellion. They had always said they would use force rather than accept home rule but did not have to plan to carry out this threat until the House of Lords lost its veto power in 1911. Bonar Law, who had become leader of the Conservative party in 1911, was particularly important in encouraging the new policy. Addressing a mass meeting at Blenheim Palace, England, in 1912, he said, "I can imagine no length of resistence to which Ulster can go in which I should not be prepared to support them, and in which, in my belief, they would not be supported by the overwhelming majority of the British people."[1]

Law and his Conservative colleagues justified their support for a unionist rebellion by insisting that they were upholding, not attacking, the constitution. In their view, the Act of Union of 1800 was a fundamental constitutional compact with Ireland that the government could not amend without a clear mandate from the people. The act had stated that Ireland and Britain would be governed by a single parliament, and home rule appeared to break this promise by removing Irish legislation to the Irish Parliament in Dublin. But Law said that he was prepared to accept the verdict of a general election on the issue. The Liberal government replied that the Act of Union would be unimpaired under home rule because the supremacy of the U.K. Parliament was unaffected. The Irish Parliament would be a subordinate legislature, and Ireland would continue to be represented in the U.K. Parliament. Liberals refused to call a general election to test public opinion on home rule because there was no way of limiting the campaign to this one issue.

Given this stalemate, the unionists proceeded to plan their last stand. Sir Edward Carson, a member of Parliament for Dublin University, not an Ulsterman himself, accepted the leadership of the Ulster unionists in the summer of 1911. Under his leadership they prepared their resistence. The Ulster Unionist Council, formed in 1905, became the hub of the movement. In September 1911 it decided to prepare a provisional government that would take control of Ulster if home rule were to become law. On September 18, 1912, almost five hundred thousand people, including virtually all of the adult Protestants in Ireland, signed the Ulster Covenant in which they pledged to oppose home rule by force.

In January 1913, a unionist militia, the Ulster Volunteer Force, was formed, and in March 1914, in what has been called the Curragh Mutiny, the officers of the Curragh army base, west of Dublin, declared that they would resign their commissions rather than be ordered to Ulster to put down a unionist rebellion. Then, in April 1914, about twenty thousand rifles were smuggled into Ireland from Germany by the Ulster Volunteers in the Larne gunrunning. Colvin described the situation these events created in Ireland in his biography of Carson:

> If we consider these two groups of events of the Curragh and Larne in March and April 1914, it will be seen that before them the British Government was armed and the Loyalists of Ulster were unarmed, and that after them the British Government was disarmed and the Ulster Loyalists were armed.[2]

The government considered the arrest of the unionist leaders, the "Ulster rabble" as they were called in the Cabinet, for these flagrantly illegal acts but rejected the idea for fear of provoking a violent response in Ulster.[3]

George Dangerfield, an influential historian, has argued that the Liberal government could have put down this incipient Ulster rebellion without great difficulty had it shown the courage to act. The Ulster Covenant, he says, "was no great threat. It committed them, at most, to a state of mind."[4] He is almost certainly wrong. No one expected half a million unionist men and women to take up arms, but a large number of unionists were prepared to fight for the union, they had the general support of the Protestant community, and the extremely efficient Larne gunrunning had provided them with more than enough weapons. Ireland appeared on the verge of a unionist-inspired civil war, and the government seemed paralyzed.

The unionists' preparations had not gone unnoticed in the south of Ireland. As we saw in Chapter 5, Irish nationalists organized a counterforce, the Irish National Volunteers, in Dublin in November 1913. These volunteers were badly financed, unlike the Ulster Volunteers who had the wealth of industrial Belfast and Conservative England behind them, but in May 1914, they imported nine hundred old rifles from Germany in a gunrunning at Howth, a northern suburb of Dublin, and a further six hundred in August at Kilcoole in County Wicklow. The unionists could certainly outgun the nationalists, but the real significance of these antiquated weapons was that they saw service in Dublin in the Easter Rising two years later. It is ironic that the nationalist gunrunning was undertaken by sympathetic Protestant home rulers, not revolutionary Catholic nationalists, and many of them were serving in the British army in World War I when the Rising broke out.

John Redmond saw the growth of the Irish National Volunteers as a threat to the authority of the Irish Party and forced a number of his nominees onto the committee of the organization with an ultimatum in June 1914. He did not know that the secret Irish Republican Brotherhood was in effective control.

By the summer of 1914 there were two rival mass movements in Ireland, nationalist and unionist, both with private armies, one determined to see that home rule would be enforced and the other determined to see that it would not. Approximately one hundred thousand Irish National Volunteers stood opposite the same number of Ulster Volunteers, but the latter had a distinct advantage in weapons. Whether the unionists were bluffing or not is still being debated, but the evidence is overwhelming that the probability of a civil war in Ireland was extremely high if Irish home rule were to become law. We simply cannot ignore the Ulster Volunteers, the Larne gunrunning, the Ulster Covenant, the pro-unionist predispositions of army officers (a large number of whom were born in Ulster), the value of the Conservative party's support, or the siege mentality in Ulster at the time. It was an incendiary situation, and in July 1914 the British Army Council recognized this by advising the government that a civil war in Ireland would tie up the entire British Expeditionary Force, the army kept in reserve in Britain for possible crises aboard, which would jeopardize the security of the British Empire.[5]

THE POLITICAL CRISIS OF 1914

As the two sides prepared themselves for war in Ireland, the third home rule bill proceeded through Parliament in London, where the government seems never to have accepted that civil war was really imminent. Prime Minister, Asquith, for example, believed that the unionists were bluffing, and that the greater danger was a nationalist-inspired civil war if home rule were denied. Nevertheless, he opened secret discussions with both sides late in 1913 to try to secure a settlement to which both could consent. At the heart of these discussions was the notion that Ireland should be partitioned, one part to be governed from Dublin and the other to continue as an integral part of the United Kingdom.

It was the Ulster unionist leader, Edward Carson, and the Conservative, Bonar Law, who raised the issue of partition, although this principle clearly implied the sacrifice of southern unionists to an Irish home rule parliament. Carson and Law proposed that all nine Ulster counties be excluded from home rule, and that these should continue to be governed from London. The two leaders later amended this to six counties because three of the nine, Donegal, Monaghan, and Cavan, had large Catholic majorities. Indeed, in the nine Ulster counties as a whole there was a small Catholic majority and the Irish nationalists held one more Ulster seat in Parliament at the time than the unionists. The six-county area still included two counties, Fermanagh and Tyrone, with small Catholic majorities. The core of unionist strength lay in the city of Belfast and the four counties of the northeast: Armagh, Antrim, Down, and Londonderry.

Informal negotiations continued until July 21, 1914, when King George V convened the Buckingham Palace Conference in a final attempt to secure an agreement. By then, the issue of partition had been refined into two formulas. The government and the Irish party proposed that the six counties should be temporarily excluded from home rule for a period of six years, after which they would be included automatically. This proposal contained an implied concession which was extremely important. At some point during the six years a general election would have to be called, and if the Conservatives won they would have an opportunity to amend home rule to the satisfaction of the unionists. This means that Redmond had opened the door just a little to the possibility of permanent exclusion for some part of Ulster. However, the Unionists rejected the proposal. They saw temporary exclusion as simply a stay of execution, and they wanted to cement the principle of permanent exclusion into the deal from the outset. Furthermore, they were not prepared to gamble on an election for two reasons. First, their allies, the Conservatives, might lose. Second, they believed that the decision on whether to go into the Irish Parliament should be made by the people of Ulster, not the United Kingdom electorate as a whole.

The unionists countered, therefore, by proposing that the six counties be permanently excluded unless they were to choose, county-by-county, to accept home rule. This, too, contained an implied concession, because if the six counties were offered a vote for or against home rule, the two with small Catholic majorities might choose home rule, which would reduce the excluded area to only four counties, the solid Protestant heartland.

Redmond may have opened the door to permanent exclusion by accepting temporary partition, but we do not know if he could have carried his party with him. The public position of the Irish party was that the permanent exclusion of any part of Ireland from home rule was unacceptable. It would mean recognizing the existence of two nations, denying the principle of majority rule for the island as a whole, and violating the unity of the Irish economy. Furthermore, there were large pockets of Catholics in even the four predominantly Protestant counties, a hundred thousand or so in Belfast alone. No matter what area was excluded, therefore, there would always be the problem of the Catholic minority in the north which no partition plan could completely solve.

Similarly, we do not know if Carson and Law could have carried their supporters with them on a plan that could have reduced Ulster unionism to four counties. Partition would also mean accepting home rule for most of Ireland, with dire consequences predicted for the future of property and the British Empire. And most important, it required sacrificing the Southern unionists who had an enormous amount of support in the Conservative Party.

The obstacles to partition were immense, but it seems obvious that some form of partition would have been preferable to a civil war, if this was, indeed, what Ireland faced. The exclusion of four counties might have minimally satisfied the unionists' demand for exclusion from the Irish Parliament without violating home rule so badly as to provoke a nationalist civil war. The excluded area would have included a substantial Catholic minority, but that could have been protected by law, including guarantees of religious freedom. Such a partition proposal could only have come from the Asquith government because neither the Irish party, which publicly claimed the whole of Ireland, nor the unionists, who publicly opposed home rule and claimed the whole of Ulster, could make the first move. We have no assurance that such a plan would have been acceptable to, or could have been forced upon, the two sides, but the issue is moot because the government did not make the offer. There is some evidence that Asquith was considering an amendment to the home rule bill in late July to permanently exclude six counties, but World War I intervened. Dangerfield argues that partition would have been "unheroic, indeed perfidious," but such a judgment must assume that the unionists had no case for special consideration and posed no serious threat to public order.[6] On the evidence we have, both assumptions are wrong.

The collapse of the Buckingham Palace Conference on July 24, 1914, left the third home rule bill intact as introduced in 1912. It had passed through the House of Commons for the third time on May 25 and had gone on to the House of Lords for the last time. There, on June 23, the government belatedly proposed an amendment to exclude six counties temporarily. This was rejected by the Lords who substituted an outrageous amendment that the whole of Ulster, all nine counties, with an overall Catholic majority, should be permanently excluded. When the government refused to accept this change, the bill was finally approved, as originally framed, over the objections of the Lords, and it received the royal assent on September 14. Home rule for a united, thirty-two county Ireland was now on the statute books. However, the United Kingdom had been at war with Germany since August 4, so the passage of home rule was immediately followed by a suspensory act that delayed its implementation for the duration of the war. Both sides accepted this arrangement in the interest of prosecuting what they hoped would be a short war, but the unionists did not intend to give up the fight. They had the period of the war to prepare another line of defense.

CONCLUSION

A turning point had been reached, then, in the summer of 1914. The conventional view is that a choice had to be made between home rule or no home rule for the whole of Ireland. There are many people who still argue, with Dangerfield, that had the government "called Ulster's bluff," the unionists would have abandoned their protest and accepted the inevitable home rule. They also argue that home rule would have solved the Irish problem. It would have been, as Redmond had promised, a "final settlement." Each of these conclusions, however, is suspect.

As we have seen, by 1914 the real choice for Ireland arguably was not between home rule for a united Ireland and continuation of the union but between civil war and a plan of exclusion for the Protestants of the northeast. In addition, the weight of evidence is that Ulster was not bluffing. Home rule could not have been imposed without an explosion in the north. Finally, in the long run we can question whether home rule would have ended the Irish problem. It was not only revolutionary and romantic nationalists who did not accept a subordinate Irish Parliament as final because many constitutional nationalists themselves wanted full independence and saw home rule as a means to that end, not an end in itself. We have also seen that the home rule bills had flaws, or at the very least weaknesses, that could have produced conflicts over the respective powers of Ireland and the United Kingdom and provoked Irish demands for full independence. Even the evident willingness of the Irish party to accept bills which gave them less financial power than they believed necessary for self-government is suspicious because it suggests that they were accepting home rule simply in order to gain a foothold on Irish independence.

The real turning point for Ireland, then, may well have been not the failure of home rule in 1914 but the failure of the Liberal government to devise and offer a reasonable plan of partition. The significance of this missed opportunity must not be underestimated. Carson, the undisputed leader of the Ulster unionists, and Law, the leader of the Conservative party, believed that the constitutional imperfections of home rule contained the seeds of future discord between Ireland and the United Kingdom. The two leaders also believed that the home rule movement was a disguised separatist movement which would take advantage of any discord to move towards Irish independence. The politicians on both sides must have known, then, that home rule might not be final. Unionists knew that by accepting home rule they were accepting the possibility that an independent Ireland would evolve in the south. But partition would ensure that if or when this came about, the unionist population of the north would be protected by being excluded. On the nationalist side, some, at least, of the Irish party must have known that they had opened the door to permanent exclusion for the north by accepting temporary exclusion for six counties because a general election during the period of exclusion could have led to a Conservative government that would make partition permanent.

In these circumstances, it seems that the solution of the Irish problem could have been close at hand in 1914, had there been time to work it out. It would have been a home rule settlement for either twenty-six or twenty-eight predominantly nationalist counties, leaving the rest of Ireland to be governed from London. When a twenty-six county plan was implemented in 1921, it was too late. By then, as we will see, the Easter Rising had taken place, home rule had been destroyed, and revolutionary nationalists would accept nothing less than Irish independence.

1 Robert Blake, *Unrepentant Tory* (New York, 1956), p. 130.
2 Ian Colvin, *Carson the Statesman* (New York, 1935), p. 376.
3 Alan J. Ward, *Ireland and Anglo-American Relations*, p. 40.
4 George Dangerfield, *The Damnable Question*, p.118.
5 Dangerfield, p. 76.
6 Ibid., p. 118.

CHAPTER 9

World War I: Britain's Weakness and Ireland's Opportunity

WORLD WAR I BEGAN FOR THE UNITED KINGDOM on August 4, 1914, and before it ended, the political scene in Ireland was transformed. Home rule was suspended, the Easter Rising had occurred, the Irish party and home rule were destroyed, and revolutionary nationalism was repositioned as the choice of a majority of the Irish people.

CONSTITUTIONAL NATIONALISM AND THE WAR

On the day before the United Kingdom entered World War I, John Redmond, the leader of the Irish party, stood in the House of Commons to pledge Ireland's support. This was a dramatic gesture because for seven hundred and fifty years it had been thought in Britain that Ireland posed a threat to its security. Henry II feared the growth of a rival Norman state in Ireland and the Tudor conquest was intended, in large part, to secure the country from Spain, which several times provided support to Irish rebels during the reign of Elizabeth I. In 1690 French troops fought with James II against William of Orange and in December 1796 fourteen thousand French soldiers sailed from Brest to support the United Irishmen, but were unable to land. A smaller expedition with about eleven hundred managed to land in County Mayo in August 1798, and another French expedition was intercepted by the British navy in October 1798.

Although these were distant events, memories of Ireland as a threat to Britain remained, and they were reinforced by the recent endorsement of the Boer cause by Irish nationalists during the Boer War of 1899 to 1902. In 1901, Lord Salisbury, the British prime minister, declared,

> We know now from our South African experiences the danger of letting Ireland have a measure of independence. We know now that if we allowed those who are leading Irish politics unlimited power of making preparations against us, we should have to begin by conquering Ireland, if ever we had to fight any other power.[1]

John Redmond quickly moved to allay these fears in August 1914, and the foreign secretary, Sir Edward Grey, admitted that "the one bright spot in the very dreadful situation is Ireland."[2] Redmond followed his speech in the House of Commons with a recruiting campaign in Ireland where, with very few exceptions, both nationalists and unionists supported the war. Indeed, in America, the old Fenian, John Devoy, bemoaned the "almost universal approval of John [Redmond]'s pledge. . . . The moral rottenness at home is the worst part of it."[3]

Few Irish Americans were as revolutionary as Devoy and few were very actively pro-German, but the first year of the war illustrated the considerable difference between the Irish in Ireland and the Irish in America. By August 1915, for example, there were 132,454 Irish in the British Army, including 77,511 Catholics and 52,943 Protestants. More than 81,000 Irishmen had volunteered since the war began, and by April 1916, the total had reached 150,183, compared to the 1,500 or so republicans who turned out for the Rising that month. There was no doubt, then, that the constitutional nationalist policy of support for the war was approved by a majority of the Irish people. In America, however, Redmond's support for the war led to the almost total collapse of the United Irish League, the organization he had led so successfully for fourteen years. By 1915 he was maintaining the organization with funds sent from Ireland, a stunning reversal of prewar financial support.

By endorsing the war, Redmond certainly did not reject Irish nationalism, although Irish Americans assumed he had. In fact, neither the nationalists nor the unionists were willing to disband their volunteer organizations during the war. When it was over the nationalists intended to ensure that home rule would be implemented as approved in 1914, and the unionists were equally determined to ensure that it would not, or certainly not without excluding the north.

The nationalists were particularly buoyant because the royal assent was given to home rule on September 14. Implementation was suspended for the duration of the war, of course, but nationalists now believed they held the advantage, and that their unqualified loyalty during the war could only strengthen their claim. As Redmond said in July 1915:

> Given these two things—Ireland doing her duty to herself in the war and Ireland doing her duty to herself in keeping her political and military organizations intact . . . there is nothing more certain in this world than that as soon as the war ends Ireland will enter into the enjoyment of her inheritance.[4]

But the longer the war lasted, the weaker Redmond's position was to become.

The constitutional nationalists suffered four major setbacks in the period before the Easter Rising. First, the Irish National Volunteers split in September 1914, with about twelve thousand reorganizing as the Irish Volunteers in October 1914, in opposition to the war under the leadership of Professor Eoin MacNeill. Whilst not supporting Germany his position was that only a self-governing Ireland should participate in the war. The majority of the volunteers, about one hundred sixty thousand, remained loyal to Redmond and the war effort and were renamed the National Volunteers, but whereas they and the Ulster Volunteers began to suffer erosion from the effects of British recruitment in 1915, the antiwar Irish Volunteers did not. They even grew somewhat, to about sixteen thousand by April 1916.

Second, the unionists strengthened their political position by joining the coalition war government that Prime Minister Asquith formed in 1915. Redmond refused to join, but Sir Edward Carson, the Ulster unionist leader, became attorney general, and when he resigned in October 1915, he was succeeded by his militant unionist colleague, Sir F. E. Smith. Fierce opponents of home rule who had been prepared to rebel against Asquith in 1914 were now inside his government, and the nationalists were not.

Third, although there was an Ulster division in the army, the War Office denied the nationalist parts of Ireland any specific recognition, such as badges or insignia. And when Redmond suggested in the House of Commons that Ireland's home defense might be entrusted to the National and Ulster Volunteers, he was ignored by the government.

Fourth, the longer the war continued, with its heavy toll of lives in France, the more necessary military conscription became, and this helped the dissidents. In any war there are people who would rather not serve in the armed forces, for whatever reason, and in Ireland the threat of conscription had the effect of encouraging membership in the Irish Volunteers, the antiwar organization. The Irish were omitted from the general conscription program of 1916, and again in 1918, because the government did not want to provoke or encourage extremism, but the conscription threat always loomed over Ireland and played into the hands of the revolutionaries.

REVOLUTIONARY NATIONALISM AND THE WAR

Constitutional nationalism suffered in the war, but revolutionary nationalism did not immediately benefit. The Irish prospered economically from food exports and expanded job opportunities, and the majority of the Catholic population appeared to support Redmond. Indeed, Ireland might well have emerged from even a long war without an internal crisis had it not been for the activities of revolutionary nationalist leaders, members of the Irish Republican Brotherhood, who penetrated the leadership of the new, antiwar Irish Volunteers.

When war was declared, the revolutionary IRB Supreme Council resolved "to work for an insurrection in arms against England to be launched at the earliest possible moment, without further provocation by England than her continued government of Ireland, and the military occupation of Ireland by an English garrison."[5] This was the position of the leadership of the Clan na Gael in the United States, too, but one could be excused for thinking it hyperbole in 1914 when, Foster records, the IRB only had about 1,660 members in the whole of Ireland.[6] An insurrection was certainly not the official position of the Irish Volunteers. Their leader, Eoin MacNeill, was not a member of the IRB and his policy was that his volunteer organization should be maintained to protect home rule, not prepare for revolution. On the headquarters staff of the Irish Volunteers, however, were three IRB members, Patrick Pearse, director of military organization, Thomas MacDonagh, director of military training, and Joseph Plunkett, director of military operations, who were secretly plotting to lead the Volunteers into an insurrection. The IRB also took control of the Gaelic League in 1915.

How seriously the IRB took its mandate to launch an insurrection was illustrated in the summer of 1915 when Plunkett made his way to Berlin by way of New York to request help from the German government. None of this was known to MacNeill, nor to two other members of the headquarters staff, Bulmer Hobson, the quartermaster, and The O'Rahilly, the director of arms. This secrecy was an absurdly clumsy arrangement for which the rebels were to pay heavily in 1916, but without it MacNeill would have prevented the Rising.

The leaders of the revolutionary Clan na Gael in America began to cooperate with the Germans on two levels as soon as the war began. They openly cooperated with German-American organizations to support U.S. neutrality and oppose any support for Britain, and they secretly negotiated with Ambassador Bernstorff and other German diplomats to secure support for an IRB-led insurrection in Ireland. In this respect they served as liaison between the rebels in Ireland and the German government.

Sir Roger Casement, a retired British diplomat sympathetic to Irish nationalism, was in the United States soliciting funds for the Irish National Volunteers when the war broke out, before the movement split. He immediately saw an opportunity to implement plans for Germany to support Irish independence which he had promoted in pamphlets before the war, and it was he who drafted a declaration of

Irish-American support for Germany which was signed by the Clan na Gael executive in August 1914. Casement and John Devoy also met with Ambassador Bernstorff to broach the idea of forming an Irish brigade from Irish prisoners of war in Germany. Financed by the Clan, Casement left New York for Berlin in October 1914, and in November he secured a German declaration of support for Irish independence. On December 28, Germany signed an agreement to equip an Irish brigade to fight in Ireland, with supporting German officers and troops, if Germany should win a victory at sea. In actuality, however, Casement's plan was a disaster because only fifty-five prisoners, of rather poor military quality, volunteered for the brigade.

Casement was an expensive ally for the Clan na Gael, which spent $10,000 on his mission from its very limited resources. John Devoy tells of sending $100,000 to Ireland during this period, but this was an exaggeration because he was worried by the shortage of money and resented Casement's drain on the Clan's resources.[7] The sum sent was probably less than half that amount. Whatever the American financial contribution may have been to the Rising, it was the only outside financial contribution of any significance the IRB received because there is no evidence that German money was sent to Ireland.

The most important problem for the revolutionaries, however, was less their shortage of money than the indifference of the Irish people towards revolution. The revolutionary nationalists were making progress in 1915, but hardly enough to encourage thoughts of a rising which had any chance of military success. MacNeill's Irish Volunteers and the small Irish Citizen Army, about two hundred strong, organized by the Irish Transport and General Workers' Union, paraded separately and carried out military maneuvers quite publicly, protected by the chief secretary's desire to avoid a confrontation or crisis in Ireland. There was also a steady stream of antiwar publications, one succeeding another as they were banned, and the government found it difficult to secure convictions from Irish juries of those arrested for antiwar activities. However, no one would have said an insurrection was imminent. Nonetheless, the leadership of the IRB were quietly preparing.

In May 1915 the IRB organized a Military Committee, later renamed the Military Council, to weld the IRB, the Irish Volunteers and

Sinn Fein into one revolutionary instrument. Then, in early 1916, the Irish Citizen Army was brought into the coalition by James Connolly, its leader. By then the IRB had already decided, in December 1915, that an insurrection should be planned for the following Easter, and Connolly agreed to participate.

The decision to stage the Rising amazed John Devoy and the American Clan na Gael. Devoy wrote later: "They did not ask our advice; they simply announced a decision already taken; so, as we had already recognized the right of the Home Organization to make this supreme decision, our plain duty was to accept it and give them all the help we could."[8] Devoy did, indeed, give all the help he and the Clan na Gael could, and it was the fault of the revolutionaries in Ireland, not the Clan, that the preparations for the Rising proved to be thoroughly confused.

PLANNING THE RISING

In February 1916, Devoy wrote to Berlin at the request of the IRB requesting an arms shipment to land in Limerick on April 21 or 22, Good Friday or Easter Saturday. He asked for one hundred thousand rifles, artillery pieces, and German officers. On March 4 the Germans offered much less: twenty thousand rifles, ten machine guns, ammunition and explosives, and no officers. The shipment was scheduled to land in Tralee Bay, on the west coast, between April 20 and 23. Devoy regarded the offer as inadequate but still believed that an insurrection could be staged. Using an alias to avoid detection, he wrote to a friend about his new "position." "The salary is not as big as I expected, but it is a living wage and I am certain I would get a raise soon when they saw I could make good."[9] Casement, by contrast, who was in Bavaria recovering from a mental and physical collapse, was completely disillusioned by the Germans. He had already written on February 2, "So full of good-will, [the Germans] are swine and cads of the first order." He believed, correctly, that their offer of support was only made to impress the Irish in America and to create "some little complication for England in Ireland."[10] He decided to return to Ireland to stop the Rising, and the Germans, without knowing his intentions, agreed to send him home in a submarine. He left Germany on April 12, three days after the arms shipment.

A series of clumsy accidents now ensured that the entire German contribution would be wasted. A communications route between Ireland and Germany, via the Clan na Gael and German diplomats in America, then via Berne or Amsterdam to Berlin, caused the final landing instructions from Ireland to arrive six days after the arms ship, the *Aud*, had left Germany. The ship traveled without a radio and could not be contacted en route. Because it arrived off Tralee on the night of April 20, the captain unaware that an arrival time of nightfall on April 23 had been requested by the rebels, there was no one to receive the cargo. The Germans waited in vain for twelve hours to be contacted and were arrested by the navy soon after setting back to sea. The ship was then escorted to Queenstown, now Cobh, near Cork, where it was scuttled by its crew on April 22, with the loss of all the supplies.

Casement himself arrived in Tralee Bay early on April 21, Good Friday, still with time to influence the Rising but several days later than he anticipated because of a mechanical breakdown that forced him to change submarines en route. He was captured, with incriminating evidence in his possession, including a dated German railway ticket, a few hours after reaching the beach from his swamped landing craft. One of his two companions, Robert Monteith, who had been sent to Germany from Ireland to command the Irish Brigade, escaped and made his way to the United States; the second, Daniel Bailey, who was a member of the brigade, was captured and cooperated with the British authorities.

These events, the products of a cumbersome communications system and human error, were disastrous, of course, but events happening in Ireland were equally unfortunate. We have already noted the distinctive character of the nationalism that Patrick Pearse shared with his IRB colleagues, Thomas MacDonagh and Joseph Plunkett. The war presented them with an opportunity to make their blood sacrifice in a fight they would almost certainly lose, and in 1915 Pearse wrote, "Ireland will not find Christ's peace until she has taken Christ's sword."[11]

Few of the revolutionaries shared Pearse's mystical vision. In the United States, Devoy and the Clan na Gael had always hoped that a rising would lead to a military victory, not a heroic defeat. In Ireland, Tom Clarke and James Connolly believed in the power of example, but not necessarily the romantic notion of the blood sacrifice. Connolly believed that the war was an opportunity to destroy capitalism and was prepared to see the struggle begin in Ireland, though he might die in the process. But it was Pearse who set the tone of the Rising, and in a memorable eulogy at the grave of O'Donovan Rossa in 1915, he said,

> Life springs from death; and from the graves of patriot men and women spring living nations. The Defenders of this Realm . . . think that they have pacified Ireland . . . but the fools, the fools, the fools—they have left us our Fenian dead, and while Ireland holds these graves, Ireland unfree shall never be at peace.[12]

Pearse and his IRB colleagues were forced to operate secretly within the Irish Volunteers because of a critical difference of opinion between themselves and Eoin MacNeill. He knew that only a minority of the volunteers were armed with rifles and that they were a very small minority in the country. He therefore favored the steady growth of volunteer strength so that, at the war's end, Britain would face a resolute body of nationalists in Ireland prepared to defend home rule. MacNeill and Redmond had not separated in 1914 because of any fundamental disagreement over home rule, but because of Redmond's active support for the war. MacNeill believed that Ireland's first duty was to itself. He knew that a military success was simply out of the question in 1916 and opposed the notion of the blood sacrifice. He would only accept that the Irish Volunteers should act during the war if the government were to attempt to suppress the movement systematically, or if an attempt were made to apply military conscription in Ireland. In these contingencies, the volunteers should resort to guerilla war and not risk a direct confrontation with the British army.

MacNeill sensed, however, that he was not in complete control of the situation. In January 1916 he asked Connolly to restrain his revolutionary zeal because he feared it might provoke the government into suppressing all nationalist activities. When rumors of an insurrection began to float MacNeill sought an assurance from Pearse that there were no plans in hand. He continued to be suspicious, however, and in a memorandum in February argued that an insurrection should only be launched if there were a real chance of success and "not merely some future moral or political advantage which may be hoped for as the result of non-success." He wrote: "I do not know at this moment whether the time and the circumstances will yet justify distinct revolutionary action, but of this I am certain, that the only possible basis for successful revolutionary action is deep and widespread popular discontent. We have only to look around us in the streets to realize that no such condition exists in Ireland."[13] On April 5 MacNeill insisted that only routine orders should be issued from the volunteer headquarters without his signature, but he could not restrain the plotters.

The IRB was determined on an insurrection at Easter, and an elaborate plan was underway to deceive MacNeill. He had already agreed that the Irish Volunteers should resist any attempt by the government to suppress the organization, so when a document was published in the press on April 19 purporting to be an instruction from the Irish administration in Dublin Castle to arrest the volunteer leaders, MacNeill agreed that preparations should be made to resist. In fact, the document was probably forged. Irish under secretary Sir Matthew Nathan only asked for permission to arrest the leaders some days later, on Easter Sunday, April 23, after Casement and the *Aud* had been captured, and he had concluded that there was a German conspiracy underway.

On April 20, one of MacNeill's supporters, Bulmer Hobson, discovered that an order had gone out for the Rising actually to start on April 23, and when challenged by MacNeill, Pearse finally revealed that such an order had been issued. MacNeill was persuaded not to countermand it because of the confusion such an order would create amongst the volunteers, and because, he now learned, German arms supplies were en route, the first MacNeill knew of any German connection. By Saturday evening, April 22, however, he realized the full dimensions of the conspiracy. He knew that the *Aud* and Casement had been captured, and that the Dublin Castle document was probably forged. Very early on Sunday morning, therefore, the planned date of the Rising, MacNeill issued a countermanding order which was carried throughout Ireland, and in an advertisement placed in the *Sunday Independent* newspaper he prohibited all volunteer maneuvers.

It would be unfair to blame MacNeill's order for the confusion outside Dublin and the general failure of the country to respond to the Rising when it did take place on Easter Monday. As Dangerfield makes clear, the rest of Ireland was woefully unprepared for a rebellion in the best of circumstances.[14] What MacNeill had done was to make sure that the Rising would not happen on Easter Sunday, but Pearse had warned that a countermanding order would not be obeyed by all volunteers, and he and his associates rescheduled the Rising for Easter Monday. As we saw in Chapter 1, they led their much depleted forces out to certain military defeat at midday on April 24, believing, in the words of the Proclamation of the Irish Republic, that "Ireland, through us, summons her children to her flag and strikes for her freedom."

CONCLUSION

The Rising certainly took the British government by surprise. At one level this could be excused. It was clear in 1915 and 1916 that the Irish Volunteers, and seditious activities in general, were growing, but there was really no widespread disaffection in Ireland, and the policy of the Irish administration, which was to contain the extremists but not force them underground, appeared to be succeeding. But an insurrection was being planned, and the government paid too little heed to the evidence.

What evidence was there? In late March, the director of military intelligence informed General Friend, the commander in chief, Ireland, that wireless interceptions indicated that a rebellion was being planned for April 22 and that a request had been made for German assistance. The navy ordered strict patrolling of the Irish coast. On April 16, naval authorities at Queenstown learned that an arms shipment and the two submarines Casement used had left Germany for Ireland. Augustine Birrell, the chief secretary, Nathan, and Lord Lieutenant Wimborne were told of these movements on April 17.

So there were certainly indications some time before Easter that something was being planned, but it is not true, as has been alleged, that the United States government alerted the British to the Rising and was responsible for Casement's capture. On April 18, 1916, American agents raided a New York advertising agency that was being used as a cover for German government activities. Papers were seized from a German diplomat, Wolf von Igel, which revealed plans concerning

Casement and the Rising. But none of this information was supplied to the British Embassy until after Casement and the *Aud* had been captured. In fact, Casement was captured by accident, and the *Aud* went undetected offshore for a day.

Even given the warnings they did have from military and naval intelligence, the Irish administration saw no reason to fear an insurrection until Easter Sunday, April 23, when they asked the chief secretary for permission to arrest the leaders of the Irish Volunteers for alleged complicity with the Germans, but they did not then prepare for the Rising that came the next day. Indeed, the capture of Casement, whom they took to be a leader, the seizure of the *Aud*, and MacNeill's prohibition of maneuvers in the *Sunday Independent* would have confirmed their view that there was no longer any danger. General Friend was allowed to take his leave in England, and the army was relaxing when the Rising broke out on Easter Monday. What no one in the administration had appreciated was the very special mentality of those who led their forces into the streets that day.

1 Ward, *Ireland and Anglo-American Relations*, pp. 265–266.
2 Kee, *The Green Flag*, p. 515.
3 Ward, p. 102.
4 Kee, p. 526.
5 Ward, p. 79.
6 Foster, p. 475.
7 Ward, pp. 72, 78.
8 Ibid., p. 105.
9 Ibid., p. 105.
10 Ibid., pp. 101–102.
11 F. S. L. Lyons, *Ireland Since the Famine* (London, 1971), p. 336.
12 Pearse, *The Best of Pearse*, p. 134.
13 F. X. Martin, "Eoin MacNeill and the Easter Rising," *Irish Historical Studies* 13: 47 (March 1961): pp. 234, 240.
14 Dangerfield, pp. 200–206.

CHAPTER 10

Sinn Fein Emerges

FOLLOWING THE FENIAN RISING IN 1867, AN IRISH magistrate who understood that revolutions thrive on martyrs cautioned the government with these words, "'Let us not re-animate the feelings of Fenianism by making martyrs and exciting sympathy in their favor."[1] The government took his advice. There were many convictions in 1867 but no executions, and consequently no martyrs. This was the government's policy, too, after the Young Ireland rising of 1848. In 1916, however, fifteen of the rebel leaders were executed within two weeks of the Rising, and in August Sir Roger Casement joined this company. Sixteen martyrs had been added to the Irish pantheon.

Does this mean that Pearse succeeded in his blood sacrifice? Had the rebels, in Pearse's words, "saved Ireland's honour"? And did the Irish nation spring from the graves of these patriots, as Pearse had prophesied? In an important sense, the answer to these questions is "yes." The Rising did inspire a war of independence that culminated in Irish independence in 1922. But the answer is also "no." The Rising alone did not produce this result. The actions of the United Kingdom government were also responsible. Wiser policies might have denied Pearse and his colleagues their victory. The Rising was, after all, widely denounced in Ireland, but the layer of Irish opposition, if broad, was rather thin, and the government had no easy task in trying to control the emotional aftermath of the Rising. In these difficult circumstances it did very poorly.

TRIALS AND EXECUTIONS

The government's first mistake was probably to execute the rebel leaders after trying them by secret courts-martial. Tom Clarke was the first to die, by a firing squad in Kilmainham prison on May 3. By May 12, thirteen others had been executed in Dublin and one in Cork. Some of the executions were particularly poignant and made a deep impression when they became known. For example, James Connolly was seriously wounded during the Rising and had to be carried to his execution on a stretcher. Joseph Plunkett, who was already dying from tuberculosis, was married in his prison cell just hours before his execution. All seven of the signers of the Proclamation of Independence were executed, and while seventy-five death sentences were commuted, this was not until Irish opinion had been deeply influenced by the executions.

The decision to execute the leaders was made in the heat of the moment, and it would have required enormous generosity for the U.K. government to forgive and forget a rebellion on such a scale at such a time. Nonetheless, the executions aroused and focused the latent hostility among the Irish toward England, the sense of "we" and "they," which had existed for so long. John Redmond, who condemned the Rising in the House of Commons on April 27, warned the government not to carry out the sentences. John Dillon, his deputy, who had witnessed the Rising at first hand in Dublin, insisted that executions would destroy the Irish Party, the party of moderation and compromise, by making martyrs of the rebels. He savagely attacked the government in the House of Commons on May 11 after his advice was rejected: "[You] are washing out our whole life work in a sea of blood," he cried, and he expressed his pride in the rebels who had fought a clean fight.[2] The Catholic bishop of Limerick condemned the government for executing the leaders before any pleas for mercy could be made.

The government further damaged the Irish party in its fight for survival by putting Sir Roger Casement on trial for treason in London in June and by entrusting his prosecution to Sir F. E. Smith, the attorney general, who had been a leading Ulster rebel in the years 1912 to 1914. Casement had actually returned to Ireland to try to stop the

Rising, but he refused to plead the truth in his defense for fear of damaging the impact of the Rising. Instead, in a dramatic speech from the dock, he challenged the jurisdiction of the court and made a bold appeal for Ireland.

Casement placed the government in an embarrassing quandary. Prime Minister Asquith and his coalition colleagues, some of whom were staunch unionists, believed that the rebels had to be punished for their treason, but it had become clear from police reports that Irish opinion was rapidly turning against the government. It had also become clear that American opinion was mostly with the rebels. Even sympathetic American newspapers, such as the *New York Times*, condemned the executions as incredibly stupid. The British ambassador, Sir Cecil Spring-Rice, wrote in May, "The great bulk of American public opinion, while it might excuse executions in hot blood, would very greatly regret an execution some time after the event. . . . It is far better to make Casement ridiculous than a martyr."[3] On July 29, the United States Senate, pressured by an American campaign to save Casement, urged the United Kingdom government to treat Irish political prisoners with clemency. The government knew that these hostile reactions in Ireland and America might impede the war effort, which depended on supplies from the U.S.A., but with opinion in Britain to consider and an example to set, the decision to proceed with Casement's execution on August 3 was made unanimously in the cabinet.

Casement had certainly not appreciated the symbolic importance of the Rising when he set out for Ireland from Germany in April. He believed it was a military madness that had to be stopped. But by going back he unwittingly became a leading actor in the drama being directed by Pearse, and he too became a martyr, the sixteenth, by his execution. His remains were belatedly transferred from London to a martyr's grave in Dublin in 1965.

ATTEMPTS TO CONCILIATE

The Easter Rising brought a new set of Irish problems that the government could not ignore. With the exception of the death of Casement, all the executions were over by May 12, and it must be said that the story thereafter is not one of unrelieved repression. Both Asquith and his successor, David Lloyd George, made conciliatory gestures towards Ireland, but without success. Between May 12 and 19, Asquith was in Ireland to investigate the Rising and on his return he asked Lloyd George, then minister for munitions, to try once more to find a solution to the Irish problem. Asquith knew that Ireland was hampering the war effort at home but he seems to have been at least as concerned with the terrible impact of the Rising and executions on American opinion. Lloyd George shared his concern. "The Irish-American vote will go over to the German side," he argued. "The Americans will break our blockade and force an ignominious peace on us, unless something is done even provisionally to satisfy America."[4]

Lloyd George had been given a daunting assignment: to solve the insoluble Irish problem in the midst of a great war and following a treasonable rebellion. Neither the nationalists nor the unionists had changed their positions. Indeed, the Rising had made them more intransigent than ever. To retain its credibility in Ireland, the Irish party found that it had to be more militantly separatist than before. The unionists were able to argue that the Rising proved conclusively the dangers to British security inherent in a self-governing Ireland. Lloyd George gave the appearance of some progress towards a solution but only by offering different terms to the two sides. John Redmond and the Irish party believed they were offered home rule subject only to the temporary exclusion of six Ulster counties. The unionists believed they were offered permanent exclusion. When the proposals were introduced into the House of Commons late in July they reflected the unionist view and were immediately rejected by the Irish party, whose credibility could only have been salvaged by the immediate introduction of the 1914 home rule act.

When Lloyd George became prime minister of a new coalition government on December 7, 1916, the Irish problem had at least three dimensions. A solution was important in itself—the problem could not be left festering. In addition, so long as the government and the military were distracted by Ireland, they were also distracted from the war in Europe. Finally, the Irish problem had an impact on relations with other countries. For example, two conscription referenda were defeated in Australia in 1916 and 1917 because of Irish-Australian opposition to the war. More important was the attitude of Irish-Americans, both before and after America's entry into the war in April 1917. President Wilson begged Lloyd George to resolve the Irish question, and when Arthur Balfour, Lloyd George's foreign secretary, visited the United States in May 1917, he reported: "The [Irish] question is apparently the only difficulty we have to face here, and its settlement would no doubt greatly facilitate the vigorous and lasting cooperation of the United States Government in the war."[5]

Lloyd George proved to be a brilliant war leader, but a solution for Ireland eluded him. At best he could give it only a small portion of his time. When it forced itself through the morass of war policy to his attention, he tended to view the problem not through his old eyes as a Welsh nationalist but through the eyes of the unionist colleagues who were in his coalition. His first major move as prime minister was to accept John Redmond's suggestion that the Irish of all parties and persuasions should be invited to a convention to try to settle the problem among themselves. It was just possible, he thought, that the Irish Convention, which convened in July 1917, might arrive at a settlement, but the worst it could do was put the problem on ice for a while. Redmond died on March 6, 1918, just before the convention completed its work.

Most of the people confined after the Rising were released before the end of 1916, but the leaders still in prison, many of whom had been sentenced to death, were released before the Irish Convention opened in an attempt to improve the climate of opinion in Ireland. The gesture proved futile when Sinn Fein, by then recognized as the political arm of revolutionary nationalism, refused to participate.

In April 1918, by a vote of 44 to 29, the Irish Convention adopted a report which closely resembled the 1914 home rule act for a united Ireland. Lloyd George deluded himself into believing that the report might provide the basis for a settlement. He overlooked the fact that Sinn Fein had rejected the convention altogether, and the Ulster unionists had voted against the report because it did not provide for the exclusion of the North. No report could have been implemented without the consent of these two militant parties who disagreed so totally, and the fact that the Irish party and the southern unionists, who had finally accepted the inevitability of Irish self-government, were in the majority of those participating had become irrelevant.

When faced with the breakdown of the convention, Lloyd George used British logic to blame the Irish as a whole for failing to agree and unionist logic to blame the nationalists in particular. "They are not satisfied with getting self-determination for themselves," he said, "without depriving others of the right of self-determination."[6]

IRISH CONSCRIPTION
AND THE COLLAPSE OF CONSTITUTIONAL NATIONALISM

Revolutionary nationalism was not crushed in the months of military rule which followed the Rising. There quickly developed, for example, what Lyons calls a "cult of the dead leaders," for whom frequent commemorative masses were offered.[7] The rebel survivors went underground, and even those in prison began to organize to strike again on their release. By the end of 1916 those who had been imprisoned without trial were free, and those who had been convicted were released in June 1917, before the Irish Convention convened. The name Sinn Fein was now used everywhere for those who supported the goals of the Rising, and not simply for the members of the organization founded by Arthur Griffith in 1905. By March 1918, there were about 1,025 branches of Sinn Fein in Ireland and 81,200 members.

There was no immediate and massive desertion to Sinn Fein, but the Irish party could only survive if the following conditions were to be met. To maintain its credibility in Ireland the party had to move into a posture of active opposition to the United Kingdom government. The old policy of moderation would not accommodate the new mood of Ireland. Also, the government could do nothing to encourage further unrest in Ireland because any worsening of the situation would benefit the extremists. Neither of these conditions was met and by the end of 1918, constitutional nationalism was a spent force.

John Redmond and his followers in the constitutional movement did attempt to satisfy the first condition, a switch to active opposition to the government. They condemned the executions and rejected Lloyd George's proposals in 1916. By 1918, they had also dropped the policy of home rule, of limited autonomy for Ireland, and they were demanding dominion status, which is to say, the virtual independence that Australia, Canada, and New Zealand already enjoyed under the Crown. But they never succeeded in building a new identity for the Irish party. Indeed, policy was less important at this stage than posture, and the greater militancy of Sinn Fein was proving to be more attractive.

Sinn Fein won its first in a series of by-election victories in February 1917 when George Plunkett, the father of the executed Joseph Plunkett, ran as an independent with Sinn Fein support in the North Roscommon by-election and defeated the Irish party candidate. He refused to take his seat in Parliament, following the policy of boycott that Arthur Griffith had laid out when he founded Sinn Fein in 1905. In May 1917, Joseph MacGuinness, who was still in prison, won South Longford with the endorsement of Dr. W. J. Walsh, the Archbishop of Dublin. In July, Eamon de Valera, newly released from prison and the senior surviving officer of the Rising, won East Clare. In August, William Cosgrave won the City of Kilkenny, and in April 1918, Dr. Patrick McCartan won North King's County, where the Irish party failed to field a candidate. Finally, in June 1918 Arthur Griffith himself won in East Cavan. The Sinn Fein winners all refused to take their seats in the House of Commons, refusing to accept the legitimacy of the U.K. Parliament.

In October 1917, Sinn Fein was formally reorganized as the official political arm of the republican movement. De Valera was elected president of the party, and its founder, Arthur Griffith, became vice president. De Valera was also elected president of the Irish Volunteers so that the political and military wings of the movement were united under a single leadership. The Irish Republican Brotherhood still existed, but de Valera, for one, refused to renew his membership in the organization.

Sinn Fein's progress did not mean that a tidal wave was yet engulfing the Irish party. The party lost six seats to Sinn Fein but managed to win a number of by-elections, too. It won South County Dublin in July 1917; South Armagh, with the aid of Unionist votes, in February 1918; Waterford in March 1918, when Captain William Redmond, John Redmond's son, won his father's seat by a large margin; and East Tyrone in April 1918. But the party was in disarray. It failed to endorse the victorious constitutionalist candidate in West Cork in November 1916 for fear that he might lose, and when de Valera won East Clare, the London *Times* of July 12, 1917, reported, "Unfortunately the constitutional Nationalists are feeble and disunited." They failed altogether to enter a candidate in North King's County in April 1918.

The second condition necessary for the survival of constitutional nationalism was that the government should not exacerbate the situation in Ireland. The fact that the military regime of General Maxwell continued to control Ireland until November 1916 did nothing to improve the atmosphere, and a midnight to 4:00 A.M. curfew was still in effect in Dublin until the end of July. Over eighteen hundred people were imprisoned without trial, and many of these were not released until December. Such policies certainly antagonized a great number of people, but the real key to the Irish nationalist state of mind lay in conscription.

As mentioned, Ireland had been excluded from conscription when it was introduced elsewhere in the United Kingdom in January 1916 because the government did not want to provoke Irish extremists. In the aftermath of the Rising, Ireland was even more sensitive, and in January 1917, the chief secretary, H. E. Duke, advised that unless Ireland were first offered home rule, Irish conscription would lead to "some bloodshed now and intensified animosities henceforward."[8] The prime minister thought likewise, or so he had already told Redmond in December 1916. On March 21, 1918, however, the Germans launched their greatest offensive of the war in France. The government believed that only a new batch of conscripts could solve the shortage of troops which had suddenly been exposed, and Ireland had the only large pool of untapped conscripts in the United Kingdom, a number estimated at about 160,000. On March 25, 1918, therefore, the government decided to introduce a bill to extend conscription in Britain and introduce it into Ireland for the first time. It argued that recruits were needed, and Ireland could no longer expect to be exempted from playing its full part in the war. This decision finally killed the Irish party. As the English historian, D. C. Somervell, concluded, "[The] German offensive extinguished the last hopes of the typically Victorian compromise of Gladstonian Home Rule."[9]

The conscription decision went against almost all the advice the government was receiving from Ireland. For example, the chief secretary, Duke, said on March 27, "We might almost as well recruit Germans."[10] The lord lieutenant, Lord Wimborne, the head of the Royal Irish Constabulary, General Byrne, the Irish lord chief justice, Sir James Campbell, the Irish attorney general, James O'Connor; and even the unionist leader, Sir Edward Carson, all advised that the value of the troops raised in Ireland would be outweighed by the costs of raising them.

As these Irish officials foresaw, the anticonscription protest from Irish nationalists was immediate, overwhelming, and unprecedented. It culminated in a remarkable meeting in the Mansion House, Dublin, on April 18, when John Dillon and Eamon de Valera led the Irish party, Sinn Fein, the Irish Catholic bishops, and the trades unions in a pledge to resist conscription. A general strike was called for April 23. Nothing did more to legitimize Sinn Fein than its membership in the coalition which was called into being by conscription.

Until 1918 the government had thought that Irish conscription could not be implemented unless home rule were in operation, and it was quickly forced back to this position by the adverse reaction in Ireland to the conscription proposal. In the last days of March, therefore, the government agreed to link conscription to some unspecified measure of home rule. In the House of Commons, Lloyd George stated that this was necessary to satisfy public opinion in the Dominions and the United States, but his primary concern was now the state of opinion in Ireland. He believed, apparently, that the report of the Irish Convention, which was due early in April, would provide the basis for an Irish settlement that would make conscription possible. The truth is that home rule was no more possible in 1918 than it had been in 1914 or 1916 because the two most important parties to the dispute, the unionists and Sinn Fein, both rejected the convention report.

When the government actually introduced the conscription bill in the House of Commons on April 9, it agreed that application of the bill in Ireland would be suspended to allow Parliament an opportunity to approve what Lloyd George termed "a measure of self-government for Ireland."[11] The bill was approved in this form on April 16 and received the royal assent two days later, but the damage had been done. The government had finally committed itself to a measure of Irish conscription that could be implemented at any time by an order in council, that is, by an order from the king without reference to Parliament, and without regard to any promises made in the House of Commons about Irish self-government. John Dillon led the Irish party out of the House of Commons, protesting that Ireland would not be seduced by a vague promise of self-government.

In the few weeks in March and April 1918 that it had taken to put conscription on the statute books, disorder had grown in Ireland, and thereafter the government continued to make mistakes. On April 11, for example, Lloyd George entrusted his Irish policy to a committee chaired by Walter Long, a Tory who had been the leader of the Ulster unionists from 1906 to 1911. Long's sympathies lay almost entirely with Ulster but he had recently become a federalist. His preference now was for an Irish settlement within the framework of a federal scheme for the whole United Kingdom. This would have required radical constitutional surgery and could certainly not be implemented in time to save conscription. In any case, Long's efforts would have been ruined by the government's decision of April 16 to send a general, Lord French, to Ireland to conduct an investigation of the state of public order. French reported back that order could be restored and conscription secured by the application of force. The Irish, he insisted, had simply been misled by a minority of radicals! French had misread the situation totally. He was an insensitive man with poor judgment who had already failed as commander of the British forces in France, but early in May he was appointed to succeed Wimborne as lord lieutenant of Ireland, and Edward Shortt replaced H. E. Duke as chief secretary. Wimborne had warned Lloyd George not to legislate Irish conscription, but Lloyd George acted on the dictum, "If you don't like the message, change the messenger." His reward for this misjudgment was that the Irish situation steadily worsened.

French, the "military governor," as Lord Wimborne called him,[12] extended martial law to most of the nationalist portions of the country and banned a host of meetings, newspapers, and organizations, including Sinn Fein and the Gaelic League, but he could do nothing to prevent the situation from deteriorating. The fact that most of Sinn Fein's leaders were arrested in May and imprisoned without trial after the government claimed to have discovered a German plot in Ireland did nothing to improve the situation. The evidence for the arrests mostly related to the period of the Easter Rising two years earlier, and could not have secured convictions in a court of law. In these circumstances, of course, home rule could never be introduced, and nor could conscription. Nonetheless, the government insisted on standing publicly by both policies, and it was still discussing them when the war ended in November 1918.

THE GENERAL ELECTION OF DECEMBER 1918

No general election had been held in the United Kingdom since December 1910, so as soon as the war ended, Lloyd George dissolved Parliament and held an election on December 14, 1918. Sinn Fein contested all but two Irish constituencies. The Irish party contested only fifty-nine constituencies in Ireland and one in England, the Liverpool seat of the veteran home ruler, T. P. O'Connor. Given the absence of competition in many seats, statistical conclusions about the results are hard to draw, but it can be said that the Irish party was not completely dismissed at the polls, as the following table makes clear. Its candidates drew a large number of votes, and they and the unionists were able to deny Sinn Fein a majority of the total vote in Ireland. The truly devastating figure, however, was the number of seats won by each party. The unionists won in Protestant-dominated constituencies, with twenty-five seats, but the Irish party won only six seats in the rest of Ireland as opposed to seventy-three for Sinn Fein. Even John Dillon, the leader of the party, was defeated by Eamon de Valera in Mayo.

General Election of 14 December 1918

Party	Total Votes	M.P.'s Elected	Candidates Entered	Unopposed	% of Total U.K. Vote
Unionist	292,722	25	38	—	2.7
Irish Party	238,477	7*	60	1	2.2
Sinn Fein	486,867	73**	102	25	4.5

*Including one seat in Liverpool
** Several candidates contested more than one seat. Sixty-nine candidates were entered.
Source: David Butler and Jennie Freeman, *British Political Facts, 1900–1960* (London, 1963), p. 122.

The Irish party was routed and quickly disappeared from view, but we cannot say for certain that nationalist electors were voting for either a republic or a revolution. They had always supported constitutionalists before, and they would again in 1922, but for the moment they had lost their belief in the party of moderation and had nowhere to turn but to Sinn Fein, the party led by the rebels of 1916. Sinn Fein had reestablished the relationship between politics and violence that had worked so well for Parnell.

CONCLUSION

Although the government made many mistakes after the Easter Rising, those made in the disastrous year of 1918 stand out. Caution should have dictated that the Irish question be left alone, but Lloyd George and the war cabinet overruled the overwhelming majority of experts in Ireland and decided on conscription. To formulate a new home rule plan, the prime minister nominated a staunch unionist, Walter Long. To quell the growing disorder in Ireland, the cabinet sent Lord French, a failed general, to impose military rule. To suppress Sinn Fein, they arrested its leaders on the unsupported pretext that they had plotted with the Germans.

The result of these misjudgments was the rapid expansion of Sinn Fein caused not by a wholesale conversion of Irish men and women to revolutionary nationalism and the principles of the Easter Rising but by a popular reaction to the government's behavior. Above all, the Irish party was brought down by conscription. The great irony is that the Irish, in the end, were never conscripted and the army managed to survive in France without them.

1 León Ó Broin, *Fenian Fever: An Anglo-American Dilemma* (New York, 1971), p. 177.
2 Cited in F. S. L. Lyons, "Dillon, Redmond, and the Irish Home Rulers," in Martin, p. 35.
3 Ward, *Ireland and Anglo-American Relations, 1899–1921*, p. 114.
4 Ibid., p. 113.
5 Ibid., p. 149.
6 Ibid., p. 203.
7 F. S. L. Lyons, *Ireland Since the Famine*, p. 381.
8 Alan J. Ward, "Lloyd George and the 1918 Irish Conscription Crisis," *Historical Journal* 17: 1 (1974), pp. 108–109.
9 D. C. Somervell, *The Reign of King George V: An English Chronicle* (New York, 1935), p. 271.
10 Ward, "Lloyd George and the 1918 Irish Conscription Crisis," p. 110.
11 Ibid., p. 114.
12 Ibid., p. 117.

CHAPTER 11

A Victory for Revolutionary Nationalism

AFTER WORLD WAR I ENDED, SINN FEIN ACCEPTED the 1918 general election result as a mandate for the establishment of a parliament for the Irish Republic which Pearse had proclaimed at the Dublin General Post Office in 1916. The party had campaigned on a platform that included Ireland's withdrawal from the United Kingdom Parliament in London, the establishment of an Irish assembly in Dublin, and an appeal to the peace conference, then about to assemble in Paris, for recognition of the Irish Republic. This program was immediately implemented.

THE CREATION OF DÁIL ÉIREANN

Sinn Fein's policy was that none of its members elected to the U.K. Parliament would take their seats. Their plan was to deny legitimacy to this parliament and establish an Irish legislature in Dublin that would try to remove Ireland from British control. For thirty-four members the issue was moot because they were in prison, but twenty-seven of those who were free assembled for the first session of Dáil Éireann, the unofficial Irish parliament, at the Mansion House in Dublin on January 21, 1919. They were known as deputies. One of the first acts of this parliament was to appoint three delegates to the World War I peace conference in Paris: Eamon de Valera and Arthur Griffith, who were in prison, and George Plunkett.

On January 22, Dáil Éireann established a government for Ireland with Cathal Brugha at its head and four other members, Eoin MacNeill, Michael Collins, George Plunkett, and Richard Mulcahy as ministers. They and their civil service department heads received salaries, and Dáil deputies drew expenses. By March, the Sinn Feiners who had been arrested in the "German plot" of 1918 had been released or, as in de Valera's case, had escaped, and fifty-two deputies were therefore able to attend Dáil Éireann on April 1 when de Valera was elected to succeed Brugha. His title was *príomh-aire*, translated as president of the Irish government, but he was effectively the prime minister.

By June 1919, Dáil Éireann had a government and seven full-time officials but it could not expect to be a very effective legislature. Though originally operating in public, the Dáil was banned by the United Kingdom government in September 1919, and it went underground. It managed to meet only six times in 1919, three times in 1920, and four times in 1921. However, Sinn Fein's sweeping victories in local government elections in January and May of 1920 gave the republicans control of local administration in most of Catholic Ireland. The Dáil Éireann Department of Home Affairs was able to introduce a court system in 1919 which effectively replaced the United Kingdom system in much of the country by the following year. Other departments—dealing with education, labor, fisheries, and trade and industry—had much less success, but the Department of Agriculture was able to set up a land bank for land purchases. The government had least success, perhaps, in its control of the republican military forces, which were still deeply penetrated by the Irish Republican Brotherhood. Oddly, the minister of defense was Cathal Brugha but the real commander of what became known as the Irish Republican Army (IRA) was the minister of finance, Michael Collins, a member of the IRB Supreme Council.

The War of Independence

As Sinn Fein made advances in the political and judicial spheres early in 1919, the military wing of the republican movement slowly began the guerilla war with Britain which was to bring independence in 1922. As we have seen, command of the IRA was complicated by the continued underground existence of the IRB, which meant that neither the government nor Dáil Éireann was ever in complete control of the military situation before the truce in 1921. The pace of the war was set by the IRB and Michael Collins.

By August 1919, the conflict was seriously under way, and in the following two years, Collins pioneered twentieth-century guerrilla war. He was a survivor of the battle at the General Post Office in 1916 during the Rising, but no military strategy could have been further removed from that experience than the war of independence. [1] The Easter Rising was a siege campaign fought from fixed positions in the center of Dublin, but Collins and his men, who were poorly armed until they captured equipment from U.K. government forces in 1919, moved in small, highly mobile units that attacked at points of weakness, generally in Dublin and the south and west of Ireland. They employed tactics of ambush, terror, intimidation, and selective brutality, against the police primarily, but also against Irish collaborators and the army. If challenged, they withdrew into sanctuaries in the countryside, mountains, or areas with sympathetic populations. J. Bowyer Bell, a specialist on such warfare, writes that Ireland was not particularly good country for guerillas.[2] It lacked good roads, its terrain was too open to provide shelter, and its wild areas lacked food supplies. It could support only a limited number of guerrillas, and indeed the IRA numbered only about five thousand hard-core fighters. Their greatest asset was the sanctuary offered by a sympathetic population. The army and police suffered from extremely poor intelligence information throughout the war because, as Townshend writes,

> Their 'intelligence gap' resulted from [the republicans'] overwhelming psychological domination of the community. The rebels of 1920 were the heirs not only to the exalted legacies of the United Irishmen and the Fenians, but also to a deeper and darker tradition of agrarian secret society terrorism.[3]

The majority of Irish Catholics may have been neither proterror nor prorepublic, but they would not betray the IRA.

The United Kingdom government fought a disorganized and unsophisticated campaign. The military and police were never properly integrated, and both used poorly trained forces. They could only hope to defeat the republicans by using overwhelming power because the task of defending all possible targets against guerilla attack and searching out the hidden attackers could only be accomplished by a large force. The army had about forty thousand and the police, with auxiliaries, about seventeen thousand, but the army commander, General Macready, wanted one hundred thousand. However, even when faced by overwhelming numbers, guerrillas are almost impossible to defeat if they operate within a sympathetic population, which was the case in Ireland.

The republicans did not anticipate a clear-cut military victory. Instead, they concentrated on propaganda and making Ireland ungovernable, hoping that the United Kingdom government would choose to withdraw. The government's military response played into the republicans' hands by transforming much of Ireland into a harsh military regime, which alienated still further the nationalist parts of the country. There were no large fixed battles, but for a country with a small population, the casualties were substantial. Lyons estimates that in 1920, 230 soldiers and police were killed and 369 wounded. In the whole period from January 1919 until a truce in July 1921, the IRA suffered 752 dead and 866 wounded.[4]

It was a war filled with incidents and personalities to fuel the folklore of Irish nationalism. In March 1920, for example, the lord mayor of Cork, Thomas MacCurtain, was murdered in his home, probably by police. His successor, Terence MacSwiney, died in prison the following October after a long and highly publicized hunger strike. A week later the British executed Kevin Barry, an eighteen-year-old student since memorialized in poetry and ballad by romantic nationalists for his role in an ambush that killed six soldiers.

In March 1920 the hated Black and Tans, a group of approximately twelve hundred auxiliary police, began to operate in Ireland. They were recruited in Britain because of the understandable shortage of new recruits in Ireland. Because of a supply shortage, they wore the khaki tunics of the army and the dark green hats and trousers of the police, giving the appearance described by their customary name. They were an undisciplined group who lashed out ferociously at the IRA in what Townshend describes as "police counter terrorism."[5] Indeed, most of the atrocities committed by government forces were attributable to these and other police auxiliaries in 1920. On November 21, for example, after twelve British intelligence officers had been murdered by the IRA in Dublin, the police turned a routine search operation of a sports crowd at Croke Park, Dublin, into a shooting spree in which twelve people were killed.

The British army was better disciplined but not immune to charges of terror and intimidation. For example, it engaged in approximately one hundred and fifty official reprisals from December 1920 until the truce in July 1921 which destroyed a large number of cooperative dairies and other buildings. These acts may have been provoked by the IRA, but one of the purposes of a guerilla campaign is always to use calculated provocation to force the government into participating in the breakdown of law and order. The government then becomes the enemy. Irish nationalists have always condemned government brutality during the war of independence, but that brutality was a sure sign that the IRA campaign of provocation was succeeding. U.K. forces were becoming the problem, not the solution, in Ireland.

Notwithstanding these drawbacks, the government could think of no policy to contain the IRA except coercion. Townshend argues:

> By and large the Cabinet adhered to the "murder gang" theory
> —the belief that the majority of the Irish people were not hostile but were terrorized by a small group of fanatics—and based on it a dual policy of 'crushing murder' while reconciling the 'moderates.' But no real attempt was made to assess the strength and outlook, or even to prove the existence, of this moderate group on which the whole policy hinged.[6]

The most conspicuous act of coercion was the Restoration of Order Act of August 1920 which suspended habeas corpus and granted considerable powers and immunities to the military, including secret courts-martial. Prior to this there had been not one conviction for murder in an Irish civilian court since the shooting began in 1919.

DE VALERA IN AMERICA

In June 1919, soon after he became the leader of the underground Irish government, Eamon de Valera left secretly for the United States where, for the next eighteen months, as the war developed in Ireland, he campaigned for the Irish republic.[7] He was introduced at gatherings throughout the country as the "president of the Irish republic," not president of the Irish government, which was his real title.

Irish-American opposition to Britain had largely been suspended during the period of America's participation in the war in 1917 and 1918, but it reemerged in 1919. Politicians throughout the United States, fed a steady diet of British atrocities and Irish sufferings by Irish nationalists, jumped on the Irish republican bandwagon. Irish-American nationalism was still led by Daniel Cohalan and John Devoy, veterans of the prewar Clan na Gael, and their new vehicle was an organization founded in March 1916, the Friends of Irish Freedom, which grew to a membership of approximately 275,000 in 1919.

As de Valera campaigned across America he and Cohalan developed a mutual antipathy. Their temperaments and their principles clashed because they represented very different interests. Cohalan had always seen the Irish problem through American eyes and believed British imperialism was as great a threat to America as to Ireland. He insisted that Irish Americans should oppose British foreign policy interests in general and Anglo-American cooperation in particular. De Valera, on the other hand, was only interested in Ireland and had no quarrel with Anglo-American harmony. He wanted Irish Americans to focus their attention on the fight for Ireland, not against Britain.

Cohalan and John Redmond had already fought over this issue between 1900 and 1914. Redmond managed to weaken Cohalan's influence by organizing the United Irish League of America, which took control of the Irish-American mass movement away from organizations like the Clan na Gael. De Valera certainly did not disagree with Cohalan over the merits of revolutionary action, but like Redmond, he challenged Cohalan's perception of Ireland's role in Anglo-American relations and his leadership of Irish America. In 1919 and 1920 Cohalan was at least as determined to defeat President Wilson's peace program and the League of Nations, which he regarded as a British plot to ensnare the U.S.A. in the defense of the British empire, as he was to win Irish independence. De Valera, by contrast, was extremely angry that the Irish Victory Fund, a very large sum of money raised by the Friends of Irish Freedom, was being used primarily in the campaign to defeat the League, not the campaign to free Ireland. De Valera never succeeded in taking control of the Friends of Irish Freedom or curbing Cohalan's activities, and Cohalan had no choice but to recognize de Valera's official standing as the representative of Irish republicanism, so their relationship was a standoff. The problem for each man was that he drew support from essentially the same pool of Irish Americans.

Cohalan had some major successes and did much to publicize Ireland's cause. For example, in March 1919, he organized a great Irish Race Convention in Philadelphia that sent three Americans to lobby the World War I peace conference in Paris. He also organized a public campaign that led the U.S. House of Representatives to approve, on March 4, by a vote of 216 to 45, a resolution asking the peace conference to recognize Ireland's claim to self-determination. The same campaign led the United States Senate on June 6 to approve, by a vote of 60 to 1, a resolution asking the American peace commission to secure a hearing for the representatives of Dáil Éireann. The peace conference never did recognize Ireland, or even discuss the issue officially, but these activities dramatized the Irish cause. The Friends of Irish Freedom were also immensely powerful in the coalition that managed to defeat the League of Nations in the Senate. In March 1920 they were rewarded when the Senate added a fifteenth reservation to the fourteen that had already caused President Wilson to abandon the League. It called for Irish self-determination.

De Valera could also claim to have succeeded in his mission. He knew that he could never win official American recognition for the Irish Republic but he was received very seriously by the press and the public as the representative of the Irish people, and he was a magnificent publicist for Ireland. The new organization which he founded to challenge Cohalan's Friends of Irish Freedom, the American Association for the Recognition of the Irish Republic, was not a great success, but de Valera was able to reestablish the United States as the major source of funding for Irish nationalism that it had been before World War I. Five and a half million dollars worth of Irish bond certificates were sold that were to be redeemed for official government bonds as soon as Irish independence was internationally recognized. The bulk of this money was tied up in American litigation after a split in the Irish republican government in 1921, caused by the Anglo-Irish Treaty, but enough of it reached Ireland to fund the activities of the Dáil and the IRA. De Valera also reestablished the bond between the Irish in Ireland and Irish-America which Redmond had lost when World War I broke out in 1914.

There was, of course, one great difference between 1914 and 1920. Redmond was a constitutionalist and de Valera a revolutionary, a survivor of the Easter Rising. However, both drew huge audiences in America, where there was little awareness of the differences between the policies of home rule and republican independence. Most Irish Americans were always willing to support a leader the Irish themselves had chosen, be it Parnell, Redmond, or de Valera.

De Valera left the United States in December 1920, but the agitation which he and Cohalan had promoted carried on. The Friends of Irish Freedom and the American Association for the Recognition of the Irish Republic both continued their work. The Committee of One Hundred on Conditions in Ireland, a group of governors, senators, congressmen, mayors, and religious leaders, published a report in March 1921 which presented a desperate account of the effects of the war of independence in Ireland. The American Committee for Relief in Ireland, with an eminent list of patrons, presented an equally dramatic account of the distress and destruction caused by the war. It raised $5.25 million for relief, a sum that went to Sinn Fein. It was clear from all of these activities that unless a settlement could be reached, the war in Ireland was going to be fuelled indefinitely by American money, and Anglo-American relations would never improve.

PARTITION

De Valera was in America when Lloyd George produced a new plan for Ireland. In November 1919 a Cabinet committee chaired by Walter Long reported:

> The Committee are agreed that in view of the situation in Ireland itself, of public opinion in Great Britain, and still more of public opinion in the Dominions and the United States of America, they cannot recommend the policy either of repealing or postponing the Home Rule Act of 1914.[8]

Instead, the 1914 act would have to be amended and the committee proposed that two home rule parliaments be established in Ireland. This proposal was presented to Parliament in the Government of Ireland Bill in December 1919, and it became law in December, a year later. Twenty-six counties were included in a Southern Ireland parliament in Dublin. Six counties, including two with nationalist majorities, Fermanagh and Tyrone, were included in a Northern Ireland parliament in Belfast.

There is no evidence that a majority of unionists wanted home rule for Northern Ireland. They would have preferred simple exclusion from home rule and continued integration in the United Kingdom, as before, the policy that Law and Carson had reluctantly come to accept in 1914. But foreign policy considerations dictated the form of partition. Britain wanted to be able to argue that self-determination had been given to the whole of Ireland, albeit in two parts. Lord Hugh Cecil recognized this when he attacked the bill in the House of Lords. "We are here face to face," he insisted, "with an attempt to satisfy foreign opinion, American opinion, opinion of the Dominions; we are not faced with any real attempt to govern Ireland."[9]

The Government of Ireland Act, 1920, was very similar to the home rule bills of 1886, 1893, and 1912, but it applied to two parliaments, not one, and a Council of Ireland, composed of representatives from both parliaments, was intended to coordinate certain all-Ireland activities and plan for the eventual unification of the country. The two parliaments would control most of their domestic affairs, but the United Kingdom would control 90 percent of Ireland's tax revenues, and the supremacy of the U.K. Parliament was explicitly affirmed in the act. Neither part of Ireland would be independent. There was no possibility that Sinn Fein would accept such a limited measure of self-government because its position was that the Irish Republic had been in existence since 1916, but the Ulster unionists did accept it because the act guaranteed that they would never be absorbed into a Dublin parliament without their consent.

Elections for the two parliaments were held in May 1921, with predictable results. Unionists won forty of the fifty-two seats in the Northern Parliament, which was opened by King George V on June 22, 1921. Sinn Fein was unopposed in all but four of the seats for the

Southern Parliament, the seats of the Protestant Dublin University, and it used the elections as an inexpensive way of selecting a new, and larger, Dáil Éireann to continue as an underground parliament. Sinn Fein members boycotted the first session of the Southern Parliament on June 28, and it was immediately suspended. Southern Ireland became a Crown colony technically, with no elected representatives in the U.K. Parliament.

THE SETTLEMENT

De Valera returned to Ireland secretly in December 1920 as the Government of Ireland Act was being passed, at a time when the United Kingdom government believed Sinn Fein was losing ground. Surprisingly, the British government welcomed his return and took pains not to arrest him, believing him to be a moderate who might accept a compromise settlement, rather than an extremist like Michael Collins. But the war did not decline in 1921. The number of IRA operations grew from three hundred a week in April to five hundred a week in May, and one-fourth of all the British casualties in the war were suffered between May 1921 and the truce on July 11.

Despite the acceleration in military operations, de Valera was open to negotiations. In May 1921, for example, he met with Sir James Craig, who was soon to become the first prime minister of Northern Ireland, but it was not until the Northern Parliament had been opened on June 22 that Lloyd George made an offer of negotiations which de Valera could accept. For the first time Britain did not require Sinn Fein to surrender before talks began, and now that Northern Ireland was permanently protected by its own parliament, Lloyd George could deal seriously with de Valera. Furthermore, the war had reached a stalemate. The government believed it could still win but only by raising the conflict to a much higher level by more than doubling the number of troops in Ireland. Before doing this it decided to try to negotiate an end to the war. De Valera accepted the offer of negotiations, and a truce was agreed for July 11. He and Lloyd George began their talks in London on July 14, 1921.

Lloyd George was prepared to offer the twenty-six counties of the south the status of a dominion under the Crown, that is, the independent status within the British Empire already enjoyed by Canada, Australia, New Zealand, and South Africa. This amounted to an offer of virtual independence, although the constitutional independence of the dominions was not clarified until 1931 in the Statute of Westminster. The British government also insisted on retaining access to certain naval facilities in the south.

The British offer required de Valera to sacrifice two goals of the Easter Rising, a united Ireland and an Irish republic. Northern Ireland would remain a separate entity with its own parliament, so unification would be denied, and the south would have to accept the king as head of state, as had the other dominions. De Valera refused these terms, although he was much more concerned with the issue of a republic than the issue of a united Ireland. He would concede at most that the Irish Republic would sign a treaty of association with the British Commonwealth which would recognize the Crown as head of the Commonwealth, not as head of the Irish state. But he had no desire to fight for a united Ireland. In August 1921 he told a private session of Dáil Éireann that he did not think forcing Ulster to join an Irish state would be successful. It would be "making the same mistake . . . as England had made with Ireland."[10] He preferred to allow each Ulster county to opt out of a republic if it so chose, which would have meant that the four predominantly Protestant counties would leave. In 1937, however, it was de Valera who placed the claim to the whole of Northern Ireland into the new Irish constitution.

De Valera chose not to travel to London in October 1921 for final negotiations with Lloyd George. He sent Arthur Griffith, Michael Collins, George Gavan Duffy, Robert Barton, and E. J. Duggan, with Erskine Childers as secretary. On December 6, after long and terribly difficult negotiations, and under extreme pressure from Britain, these representative signed an agreement, commonly known as the Anglo-Irish Treaty, which accepted the essentials of Lloyd George's first offer to de Valera. There would be an independent, twenty-six-county, Irish Free State with dominion status under the Crown and a governor general. In addition, the United Kingdom would retain naval facilities in the new state. The only significant concession by Lloyd George, one that certainly helped the republicans to agree, was that a boundary commission would be convened to review the line of the Northern Ireland border with the Irish Free State.

The Irish were persuaded by Lloyd George that their refusal to sign would lead to a full-scale war in Ireland which would destroy republicanism. They yielded, and a settlement was reached, but it was not the settlement which would bring peace to Ireland. Indeed, a great tragedy was in the making. The republicans were about to fight each other in a civil war over the terms of the treaty. Ironically, Michael Collins, the military commander who was considered an extremist by the United Kingdom government in 1920, accepted the settlement, and de Valera, the ostensible moderate, rejected it.

Griffith, Collins, and their colleagues on the negotiating team believed that they had legal authority to sign the treaty in London on behalf of the Dáil Éireann government, but de Valera insisted that they should first have sought the approval of the full republican government in Dublin. When the agreement was considered by that government a few days later it was approved by only four votes to three, with de Valera, Cathal Brugha, and Austin Stack, none of whom had been in the negotiating team, insisting that Ireland should fight on. In the majority were Arthur Griffith, Michael Collins, William Cosgrave, and Robert Barton, three of whom had been in London. Their view, argued most strongly by Griffith and Collins, was that Lloyd George and the government simply would not concede either a united Ireland or a republic. The IRA had forced Britain to negotiate but it could not win a military victory for Ireland. The treaty was, therefore, the best deal that could be secured in the circumstances. It recognized nationalist Ireland's right to self-government and legal equality with the other dominions within the Commonwealth and provided the basis for the full freedom that would ultimately come. Collins insisted that the treaty was "not the ultimate freedom that all nations aspire and develop to, but the freedom to achieve it."[11] In Collins's favor, it must be argued, was the promised boundary commission, which he and his protreaty colleagues believed might so reduce the size of Northern Ireland that it would soon choose to join the south.

The close division within the government was reflected in Dáil Éireann on January 7 when the treaty was approved by a narrow margin of sixty-four votes to fifty-seven. De Valera then left the Dáil temporarily with his supporters, and Arthur Griffith was elected to replace him as leader of the Dáil government. The way was now open to implement the treaty, but the United Kingdom refused to recognize Dáil Éireann as a parliament or Griffith as the leader of its government. It therefore resorted to constitutional sleight of hand. The Southern Ireland home rule parliament was convened with one purpose, to appoint Michael Collins to head a provisional southern administration which would deal with the transition to the Irish Free State. Griffith remained as head of the unrecognized Dáil government, but he and Collins prepared side by side for the difficult transition to the new Irish Free State, effectively as joint chief executives. The process proved to be a stormy one.

Collins and Griffith worked desperately for a compromise with de Valera that would allow him to support the treaty and the new state, but without success because they could only secure his cooperation by writing a Free State constitution that would have violated the treaty and alienated the British. The general election of June 24, 1922, which was to elect the first Dáil Éireann of the Irish Free State, was therefore fought on the issue of the treaty. The protreaty republicans won fifty-eight seats with 620,283 votes and the antitreaty side won thirty-five seats with 133,864 votes. The remaining 247,226 votes were shared between the Labour Party, with seventeen seats, independents and farmers with seven seats each, and Dublin University, with four seats. When these minor parties and independents were included, the protreaty forces had won a more than 2.5 to 1 majority in seats, and a huge 6.5 to 1 majority in votes. The results were clear to all but the antitreaty republicans.

THE CIVIL WAR

De Valera's republicanism had been defeated in the treaty negotiations, the government, and Dáil Éireann, and now, decisively, at the polls, but the first shots had already been heard in the civil war. De Valera predicted war if his demands were not met, but he was not really in control of the republican extremists. Instead he followed in their wake. In actions reminiscent of the Easter Rising, an antitreaty group occupied the Four Courts in Dublin in April and were still there during the election in June. Collins's decision to dislodge them on June 28 marked the first major confrontation of a civil war.

The war took the form of sporadic guerilla attacks and reprisals. It was fought, initially, between the protreaty and antitreaty factions of what had become the Irish Republican Army during the war of independence, but the protreaty forces were soon formally reorganized as the Irish Free State army, which grew to about thirty-five thousand men. The antitreaty republicans numbered about eight thousand when they were forced to surrender on May 24, 1923. By then approximately five hundred people had died and about thirteen thousand republicans had been taken prisoner. Seventy-seven republicans had been executed in less than a year of war, compared with only twenty-four executions carried out by the British in two years of the war of independence, in 1920 and 1921. It had therefore been a savage war, but not, it now appears, an unusual one. Desmond Williams observed that civil wars commonly follow revolutions conducted in the name of liberty, in France and the Soviet Union, for example. Such wars share a common pattern. As Williams writes, "The old order is gone; the new one waits to be shaped . . . in such wars the parties and persons involved think they have a monopoly of righteousness. Human life has less value, for those engaged grow used to giving and taking death as the fever proceeds."[12]

The Early Years of an Independent Ireland

Ireland paid a very heavy price for the civil war. There were, of course, the dead and the wounded and the normal material losses of any armed conflict, but there were also deep psychological wounds. This was a civil war between enemies who had recently been friends and colleagues in a war of independence. But, as Williams points out, "When friends fall out, the daggers stay sharp."[13] Their quarrel was over the most fundamental revolutionary principle, the legitimacy of the Irish Republic that Pearse had declared at the GPO in 1916. Collins and Griffith could argue perfectly reasonably that the 1921 settlement was militarily necessary and politically prudent, but de Valera could take the revolutionary high ground by accusing them of betraying the republican ideal. Pearse, Connolly, and the rest surely had not died so that Ireland could have dominion status and an oath of allegiance to the king. As de Valera said during the treaty debate, "I am against the Treaty because it does not do the fundamental thing."[14] Ireland was a historic nation, not a British settlers' dominion like Canada.

The issue of the betrayal of the republic was central in the debate on the treaty, and the failure to secure a united Ireland, though important, was of secondary concern. Dangerfield has argued that if the Irish delegation had refused to sign the treaty in London and had remained faithful to the republic, "It is as certain as anything can be that there would have been no war."[15] By this interpretation, the British were bluffing when they threatened to resume the war and the Irish negotiators who signed the treaty in London, Griffith, Collins, Duffy, Barton and Duggan, become responsible for the civil war because they did not have to sign the treaty. It follows that if they had not signed, there would have been no need for de Valera and his supporters to reject the treaty, and there would have been no civil war.

The following points can be made in response to this interpretation. Collins was a very hard man and nobody's fool. As commander of the IRA he had arguably done more than any other individual to bring Lloyd George to the negotiating table, and he had no doubt that Lloyd George was not bluffing when he threatened to resume the war. Collins's colleagues in London agreed, and the call was surely theirs to make. Also, whether the British were bluffing or not is in a very important sense irrelevant, from a democratic perspective. Consider the following sequence. Collins, Griffith and their colleagues believed that the British would resume the war if they did not sign a marginally acceptable treaty, so they signed. Then, the treaty was accepted by a four to three majority of the Irish republican government and by a 64 to 57 majority in Dáil Éireann. Finally, it received more than six times as many votes as the antitreaty position in the June 1922 Dáil general election. The decision to accept the treaty was therefore approved at every level of responsibility in the nationalist community, from the Irish delegation in London to the Irish people in a general election, and all points in between. By this democratic interpretation, the antitreaty faction must be held responsible for the war.

Two very revealing quotations illustrate the two sides of this debate. The first is by Collins, supporting the treaty: "It is for the Irish people—who are our masters, not our servants, as some think—it is for the Irish people to say whether [the treaty] is good enough."[16] The second quotation is by de Valera, opposing the treaty: "The Majority have never a right to do wrong."[17] Charles Townshend described the Easter Rising as "the armed propaganda of a self-selected vanguard which claimed the power to interpret the general will,"[18] but the general will was actually confirmed retroactively in the general election of 1918 when Sinn Fein won so decisively. By the summer of 1922 the general will had been ascertained again, in the general election, and it quite clearly favored Collins.

The treaty was certainly not perfect, but with the benefit of hindsight can we say whether it was worth having? The evidence suggests that Collins was right. The treaty provided for a twenty-six county Irish Free State, essentially independent, with the constitutional status of a dominion of the British Commonwealth, like Canada. There were ambiguities and uncertainties, of course, particularly the constitutional meaning of a dominion and the future boundary of the state, but in the following years all but one of these problems, the boundary issue, was resolved peacefully in favor of the new Irish state.

The Statute of Westminster, adopted by the U.K. Parliament in 1931, made clear that Britain and the dominions were legally co-equal in the Commonwealth and each fully sovereign. The Irish government of William Cosgrave was extremely important in Commonwealth meetings in promoting this clarification. After de Valera himself became prime minister of the Irish Free State in 1932 he used the Statute of Westminster as legal support for Ireland to abolish the oath of allegiance to the king, and there was nothing the United Kingdom could do about it. Early in 1937, the Free State removed all references to the Crown from the Free State constitution, other than to recognize that the king would act for Ireland in foreign affairs, which de Valera wanted to retain because he did not want to sever Ireland's link with the British Commonwealth at that time. Later in 1937, Ireland adopted a completely new constitution that was fully republican in form. The name of the country was officially changed to Eire. In 1938, after negotiations, the United Kingdom abandoned its rights to naval bases in southern Ireland. Finally, in 1949 Eire formally adopted the name, the Republic of Ireland, and withdrew from the British Commonwealth. In the same year, India became a republic and remained within the Commonwealth, a formula de Valera had suggested for Ireland in 1921, when he called it "external association." Lloyd George rejected the proposal at that time but it was revived for India. In 1949, however, the Irish Republic no longer had an interest in being in the Commonwealth. As Desmond Williams put it, "By the time the British found the answer, the Irish had lost interest in the question."[19] It was ironic that this final step to an Irish republic was taken by a coalition government led by Fine Gael, the party which had evolved from the protreaty faction of 1922.

The one great disappointment for Irish nationalists in this list of constitutional successes was that the boundary commission for which the protreaty faction had high hopes in 1922 was a huge disappointment. The commission ruled in 1925 that there should be no substantial alteration in the border with Northern Ireland. It was composed of a unionist, a South African judge, and Eoin MacNeill, who represented the Free State. MacNeill dissented in the 2 to 1 ruling but the Free State was forced to accept the existing partition with the north.

In hindsight we can agree that there were good and bad effects flowing from the treaty. Supporters of the antitreaty faction might still want to argue that the bad—the failure of the boundary commission—justified the civil war, but this argument lost its force in 1926 when de Valera, who was in a Free State prison until 1924, formed a new party, Fianna Fáil, and began to participate in democratic politics. He left behind a small republican faction in Sinn Fein and the IRA who refused to give up the struggle for a republic, and in their eyes de Valera, like Collins and Griffith, betrayed the republican ideal. But in 1927, Fianna Fáil contested a general election, won forty-four seats, and took its seats as the second largest party in Dáil Éireann. De Valera even signed the oath of allegiance to the Crown, although he argued that it was just a meaningless set of words.

In 1932 Fianna Fáil won seventy seats in a Dáil general election, enough to form a government with Labour Party support, and de Valera became prime minister of the Irish Free State just ten years after he had participated in a civil war to prevent its coming into existence. Subsequently his government removed the oath of allegiance and wrote the 1937 constitution. It was also his government that banned the IRA in 1936 and suspended normal legal processes so as to suppress the organization during its campaign of dynamite sabotage in Britain in 1939. By the end of World War II, his government and the governments of Northern Ireland and the United Kingdom, had combined virtually to destroy the IRA. The knowledge that de Valera and most of his antitreaty supporters had accepted the Irish Free State in 1927, though under protest, had come to govern it in 1932, and had used the powers of the state to suppress the remnants of the antitreaty IRA makes it extremely difficult to condone their support for civil war in 1922. Their only excuse is that they acted in stubborn good faith.

CONCLUSION

The civil war had a profound effect on Irish political life. As one example, Fine Gael and Fianna Fáil, the two major political parties in contemporary Ireland, are the descendants of the pro- and antitreaty factions respectively. Both have changed with the times, but the relatively non-ideological character of Irish politics is due largely to the fact that for many years the fundamental cleavage in the political system was not based on class, interest, or ideology, but on the memory of the civil war and which side one, or one's parents, took. Many people who served in that conflict only passed out of Irish public life in the 1960s and 1970s. De Valera himself died in 1975. In the long struggle between the two groups, the antitreaty faction has achieved the greatest electoral successes. De Valera, for example, served as prime minister from 1932 to 1948, 1951 to 1954, and 1957 to 1959, and as president from 1959 until 1973.

De Valera's success was certainly due in large part to his exceptional abilities and his willingness to change, but it might also have been due to the events of August 1922. In that month, both Arthur Griffith and Michael Collins, by then the elected leaders of the new Ireland, died. Griffith's death was from natural causes on August 12, probably hastened by the pressures of the time. Collins was gunned down by antitreaty forces in an ambush just ten days later when he was touring his native County Cork. He was a young man, still two months short of his thirty-second birthday, yet he was an authentic hero who stood well above de Valera at the time in the eyes of Irish nationalists. He had the courage to associate himself with moderation and compromise, although he predicted when he signed the treaty in London that it would cost him his life.

The deaths of Collins and Griffith, left a great void in Ireland. They were succeeded as protreaty leaders by people with impeccable republican credentials. William Cosgrave, who became the first prime minister of the Irish Free State when it was formally inaugurated in December 1922, had been condemned to death for his part in the 1916 Rising, and his deputy, Kevin O'Higgins, had been imprisoned in 1918, but neither man had the reputation or the charisma of Michael Collins. Furthermore, in 1927 O'Higgins was also assassinated, at the age of thirty-five. De Valera, on the other hand, survived to a venerable old age. He was able to fashion a very different image of himself and the civil war from what had existed in the early 1920s, and he redeemed himself in the eyes of the majority of his countrymen. But his enemies never forgave him.

1 Charles Townshend, *The British Campaign in Ireland, 1919–1921* (London, 1975), p. 66.

2 J. Bowyer Bell, *The Secret Army: A History of the I.R.A.* (Cambridge, MA, 1970), p. 23.

3 Townshend, pp. 63–64.

4 Lyons, *Ireland Since the Famine*, p. 415.

5 Townshend, p. 113.

6 Ibid., p. 203.

7 De Valera's visit to America is described in Ward, *Ireland and Anglo-American Relations*, Chap. 10.

8 Ibid., p. 227.

9 Ibid., p. 226.

10 Cited in C. C. O'Brien, *States of Ireland* (New York, 1972), p. 295.

11 Lyons, p. 442.

12 Desmond Williams, ed., *The Irish Struggle, 1916–1926* (London, 1966) p. 117.

13 Williams, p. 118.

14 Cited by Nicholas Mansergh, "Ireland and the British Commonwealth of Nations: the Dominion Settlement," in Williams, p. 138.

15 Dangerfield, p. 345.

16 Donal O'Sullivan, *The Irish Free State and its Senate* (London, 1940), p. 52.

17 Ibid., p.57.

18 Townshend, p. 312.

19 Williams, p. 139.

CHAPTER 12

The Effects of the Rising

THE EASTER RISING OF 1916 SET IN MOTION FORCES that led to the creation of an independent Irish Free State in 1922. As we saw in Chapter 10, it is not certain that this had to be the outcome of the Rising, but given the response of the United Kingdom and the circumstances of World War I, it is what actually happened. Independence might have been a joyful occasion but the victory was a hollow one because the Irish Free State celebrated its birth with a civil war between people who had very different notions about what had been achieved. On the one hand, the protreaty faction, anxious to avoid a continuing a war with Britain that could not be won, accepted the Anglo-Irish treaty of December 1921 and the Irish Free State as the best that could be secured at the time. On the other hand, the antitreaty faction decided to fight on for full recognition of the Irish republic that had been declared at the Dublin GPO in 1916. The two sides disagreed fundamentally, although neither believed that the 1921 treaty was a great one for Ireland. Both were disappointed, and they might be disappointed still were they to take literally the promise of 1916. The men and women who staged the Easter Rising hoped for much more, as they needed to, perhaps, to justify their sacrifice. Pearse, for example, died for four things: an independent, republican, Gaelic, and united Ireland. Two of these have been achieved, independence and a republic, but Ireland today is neither Gaelic nor united. James Connelly died for a socialist Ireland, and he, too, would be disappointed.

THE UNFINISHED REVOLUTION: A GAELIC IRELAND

A Gaelic Ireland was particularly important to Pearse because he and other romantic nationalists believed the key to rediscovering the historic Irish nation lay in the Irish language, a form of Gaelic. Many of the leaders of the Rising, including Pearse himself and de Valera, came into the nationalist movement by way of the Gaelic language revival, and it is not an exaggeration to say that without the Gaelic League there would have been no Easter Rising. Pearse himself wanted to achieve an Ireland which was "not free merely, but Gaelic as well; not Gaelic merely, but free as well."[1]

A French visitor to Ireland in 1790 noticed that "a great deal of Irish is spoken but nowhere does one see *notices* in Irish, as no one knows how to read it."[2] He was witness to the fact that, with the exception of poetry, the dominant public language of Ireland was already English in the late eighteenth century. The Gaelic revival sought to revive Irish in the late nineteenth century as the key to creating an Irish national identity, and after 1922 the Irish Free State accepted this as official policy. Article 4 of the 1922 constitution recognized Irish and English equally as national languages, and under the leadership of the first minister of education, Eoin MacNeill, Professor of Early Irish History at University College, Dublin, the study of Irish was made compulsory in Irish Free State schools. Article 8 of the 1937 constitution subsequently recognized Irish as the first official language of Ireland, and English as the second.

Despite this commitment to Irish, the primary language of instruction and communication in Ireland, even in Parliament, the *Oireachtas*, is still English. There are books, plays, magazines, newspapers, and television and radio programs in Irish but they serve a minority audience, although more Irish men and women read and speak at least some Irish now than before independence. The 1996 census recorded that 41 percent of Irish people over the age of three could speak Irish, about two-and-a-half times as many as in 1926, but the highest proportion in any region, 76 percent, was in the *Gaeltacht*, or Gaelic areas, which receive special protection from the state, and about two-thirds of Irish speakers were in the ten-to-nineteen age cohort, and therefore generally still attending school. Indeed, of the 25 percent who spoke

Irish daily, nearly 79 percent were in school. So in 1996, as in the early years of the Irish Free State, schoolchildren bore the brunt of the official Irish language policy.

There is a flourishing Irish culture in music, dancing, and sports, all of them rediscovered in the latter part of the nineteenth century, but Ireland does not, and in an age of television and the Internet cannot, exclude activities with English origins. In sports, for example, the Irish Republic soccer team qualified for the World Cup finals in 1994, to great acclaim, and the country gives good support to the all-Ireland rugby union team which plays at Lansdowne Park, Dublin. There is also, of course, a rich and substantial Irish literature in the English language. Four Irish-born writers who work in English have won the Nobel prize for literature: William Butler Yeats (1923), George Bernard Shaw (1925), Samuel Beckett (1969) and Seamus Heaney (1995). Three were from the Protestant community in the south, and one, Heaney, is from the Catholic community in the north, but all four are acclaimed as Irish native sons. Ireland is very important in the English-speaking world, and complete success for a Gaelic revival would isolate the country culturally, as Daniel O'Connell, an Irish speaker, warned in the early nineteenth century.

THE UNFINISHED REVOLUTION: A UNITED IRELAND

The Easter Rising was also fought for a united Ireland. Those who signed the Anglo-Irish treaty hoped for the peaceful unification of the country and anticipated that the promised boundary revision would contribute to this end by reducing the north to an impractical size. The boundary commission was a great disappointment to the south and did nothing to advance the cause, but there were at least six other reasons why unification was even less likely after 1922 than before.

First, Irish nationalist attitudes to foreign affairs distanced the Irish Republic from Northern Ireland. The Easter Rising and the anticonscription movement were seen from the north as evidence of Irish disloyalty during World War I, and unionist suspicions were compounded by Irish neutrality in World War II. Notwithstanding the threat to European civilization posed by Hitler and Mussolini, de Valera and his government had widespread popular support when they refused to commit Ireland to the war because their country was not yet, in their view, free itself. Irish neutrality was relatively benevolent, but it was neutrality nonetheless, and it was followed in 1949 by Ireland's refusal to sign the North Atlantic Treaty and its withdrawal from the British Commonwealth, both of which further distanced the country from the north.

Second, the cumulative violence of the Easter Rising, the war of independence, and the civil war, spread over a period of about seven years, from 1916 to 1923, reached into the north and frightened unionists there. The revolutionary leaders who emerged after 1916 were far more terrifying neighbors than even the rather moderate constitutional nationalists had been before, and periodic violence by the IRA in the years since 1923 has done nothing to reassure unionists.

Third, the new Irish state was born of the Easter Rising, and its patriotism, myths, heroes, and civic values were those of the men and women of revolutionary tradition: Tone, Emmet, Pearse, Connolly, Clarke, Markiewicz, Casement, de Valera, Collins, and the rest. These names, and what they represented, were antithetical to the values of unionism, with its loyalty to the Crown and the British Empire. The intensity of the celebration of the fiftieth anniversary of the Easter Rising in 1966, in both the Irish Republic and nationalist communities in Northern Ireland, strengthened unionist resolve to resist change just at the time when a Catholic civil-rights movement was making perfectly defensible claims for reform in the north.

Fourth, an autonomous political system was created in the north in 1921 which the unionists quickly realized they could dominate. Article 44 of the Irish Free State constitution permitted the Northern Ireland Parliament to vote to become a subordinate parliament of the Free State, rather than the United Kingdom, but it rejected this option on December 7, 1922, two days after the Free State came into existence. Unionists in the northern parliament knew that they had unprecedented control of most of their domestic affairs, with the full backing of the United Kingdom, and they were not about to give this away.

Fifth, Irish nationalists in the north and the south consistently denied the legitimacy of the Northern Ireland Parliament. In the north nationalists elected to parliament refused to take their seats until 1925 and were always regarded as agents of the south by unionist politicians. In the south, nationalists insisted that an Irish Republic had been proclaimed for the whole of Ireland in 1916, and although this fiction was abandoned for a while in the 1922 constitution, which was drafted to satisfy Britain, it was revived in de Valera's 1937 constitution. Article 2 declared, "The national territory consists of the whole island of Ireland. . . ." Article 3 recognized that Northern Ireland was not yet integrated into the Irish state, but Article 2 was a constant irritant to the north because it meant that unification would come on the nationalists' terms. The people of the north appeared to have no rights in the matter. Articles 2 and 3 were removed from the Irish constitution by referendum, but only in 1998, following the Belfast Agreement, as part of the Northern Ireland peace process. The removal had been suggested as early as 1967 by an official committee that reviewed the constitution, but Fianna Fáil was slow to agree. Nonetheless, in an interesting sign of the times, it was the Fianna Fáil–led coalition government of Bernie Ahern that signed the Belfast Agreement in 1998 and put the referendum on Articles 2 and 3 to Irish voters.

Sixth, the policies of the new Irish state were antithetical to unionism in two important respects. The first concerned the Irish language and the second the Roman Catholic Church. Douglas Hyde, the Protestant founder of the Gaelic League and president of Ireland from 1938 to 1949, explained why he tried to keep the league out of politics. "My ambition," he said, "had always been to use the [Irish] language as a neutral field upon which all Irishmen might meet...."[3] He was being naive because, apart from a handful of romantic nationalists like himself, Irish Protestants had no interest in the Gaelic tradition, and the adoption of Irish language policies by the Irish Free State did nothing to endear unification to the majority in the north. Indeed, no nationalism that defined itself in Gaelic terms could form the basis for a united Ireland. Garret FitzGerald, who was later to become prime minister of Ireland, recognized this in his book, *Towards a New Ireland*, in 1972:

> The new nationalism created by 1916 owed much of its strength—perhaps even its existence—to the language movement of the late nineteenth and early twentieth centuries. In

seeking to repay this debt, and, indeed, in seeking to give con-
crete shape to the aspirations of the men of 1916 who had
been trying to re-kindle what they felt to be a dying nationalism, those who inherited the mantle of the executed leaders
did in fact create a new Ireland much more alien to the Northern Protestants than the kind of Ireland that had existed before the Great War.[4]

Closely associated with the concept of a Gaelic Ireland was the
concept of a Catholic Ireland. Unionists always feared that a Dublin
parliament would be an instrument of Catholic oppression. Home
rule would mean Rome rule! They were wrong. Since independence
the Protestant minority in the south has been treated with respect by
the southern state. This may be because their small numbers, only 10
percent in 1922 and now down to less than 5 percent, and their acceptance of an independent Ireland once it was inevitable, meant that
they posed no threat to the state. Freedom of religion was guaranteed
in the Northern Ireland constitution in 1921, and in both the 1922
and 1937 Irish constitutions, but whereas freedom of worship has always been respected in both parts of the island, southern Protestants
have felt very much more secure in nonreligious aspects of their lives,
in their employment, for example, than have Catholics in the north.
By contrast, two Protestants have been president of Ireland, Douglas
Hyde from 1938 to 1949, and Erskine Childers, from 1973 to 1974. In
the half century of self-government, from 1921 to 1972, only one
Catholic ever served in the Northern Ireland government, and then
only as a junior minister in the Prime Minister's office.

Despite the evident toleration of non-Catholics in the south, it is
the case that the Irish state has incorporated Catholic doctrine into its
constitution and law several times since 1922, and this has provided
ammunition to unionist critics. For example, Article 44.2.1 of the 1937
constitution recognized the special position of the Roman Catholic
Church as guardian of the faith of the Irish majority. This was removed
by a referendum in 1972 after it was realized that it could be read as
meaning that Catholics would have a privileged status in a united Ireland. In fact, the article simply recognized the reality of a Catholic
majority and gave them no special privileges, but its removal, with the
approval of the Catholic Church, was an important symbolic act.

There remained other parts of Irish constitutional and statute law that were more than symbolic because they incorporated Catholic doctrine in law. Article 41.3.2 of the 1937 constitution, for example, forbade divorce. The prohibition was removed by a wafer-thin majority of less than .5 percent in a 1995 referendum, marking the first major defeat for the church in modern Ireland. Irish law also banned the sale of contraceptives until allowing limited sales to married couples in 1979. Only in 1992 did contraceptives become freely available. Abortion, too, is constitutionally prohibited and likely to remain so. Finally, for many years Ireland had a particularly stringent censorship of books, tightly monitored by the church, which at one time led to the banning of a huge list of the twentieth century's greatest writers, including, for example, William Faulkner, André Gide, Graham Greene, Ernest Hemingway, H. G. Wells, and Tennessee Williams, to name just a few. Censorship is not an exclusively Catholic phenomenon, but the Irish Catholic Church seriously impeded changing literary and moral standards in Ireland until changes in the censorship law in 1967.

Despite this evidence that Catholic doctrine was sometimes written into Irish law, the relationship between the Roman Catholic Church and the state has been distorted. Conservative moral standards in the north, largely set by a very conservative Presbyterian church, have been rather like those in the Catholic south. There are, furthermore, very few examples of the Catholic Church actually issuing directives to an Irish government. One case, when the government yielded to church pressure in 1951 and abandoned a scheme to provide free medical care to mothers and children, is so frequently the only example cited that we can be sure it does not happen very often. The church took this extraordinary position because it feared the state would weaken church influence in family life. But looking for church directives to politicians really misses the point. The great majority of Irish politicians are devout Catholics, and they legislate as such. Much the same can be said of conservative Protestant politicians in Northern Ireland.

In 1932, Eamon de Valera admitted that the only way to end partition was "to use such freedom as we can secure to get for the people in this part of Ireland such conditions as will make the people of the other part of Ireland wish to belong to this part."[5] In practice this did not mean he would change Irish language policies or reduce the Catholic influence over Irish law. In a 1939 radio broadcast, de Valera said,

"We are a Catholic nation."[6] This was in some ways the mirror image of the Protestant view of Northern Ireland as a Protestant state, but there was a significant difference. The Irish Republic claimed the north. Northern Ireland did not claim the south.

Politicians in the Irish Republic only began to wake up to the fact that their domestic policies were at odds with their claims to the north about forty years after W. B. Yeats, Ireland's foremost poet, a Protestant, and by then a member of the Irish Free State Senate, had begged his colleagues, unsuccessfully, not to impose their moral values on the Protestant minority.[7] Yeats may have been expecting too much tolerance from a brand new country with a Catholic majority of 90 percent, but as Professor J. C. Beckett, a northern Protestant historian, pointed out in 1976, for the Irish state "to demand territorial unity while emphasizing cultural division was an irresponsibly dangerous policy."[8] It certainly did nothing to hasten a united Ireland.

THE UNFINISHED REVOLUTION: A SOCIALIST IRELAND

The visions of a Gaelic and united Ireland have gone unfulfilled, but so too has James Connolly's dream of a socialist Ireland. Connolly led the Irish Citizen Army in the Rising and was executed in 1916, but his basic values were not those of his revolutionary colleagues raised in the Gaelic tradition. He hoped that the rebellion would lead the way to the establishment of socialism all over Europe, but although the Proclamation of the Irish Republic made references to equality and to "the right of the people of Ireland to the ownership of Ireland," these concepts could be interpreted in nonsocialist terms. When the first session of Dáil Éireann endorsed a "Democratic Program" in 1919 it was radical in the context of its time but not socialist. It supported trade unions and the principle of public ownership of parts of the economy, and it guaranteed that "no child shall suffer hunger or cold from lack of food, clothing or shelter," but it was principally a platform for the welfare state and the mixed economy that Ireland has become under a series of nonsocialist governments.[9]

With the major exception of Connolly, the leaders of the Easter Rising and Sinn Fein were bourgeois and middle class, not working class and socialist. When the Irish Labor Party, which represented the Irish working class, decided not to run candidates against Sinn Fein in the general elections of 1918 and 1921 for fear of weakening the nationalist vote, it permanently damaged its future in Ireland. The party finally decided to contest the general election in 1922 only to find that it was fought on the issue of the Anglo-Irish treaty. Labor won only 17 of 142 seats and was squeezed out in the bitter struggle between the protreaty and antitreaty republicans. These factions evolved into the two major parties of postindependence Ireland, Fine Gael and Fianna Fáil respectively, and in place of the politics of class, which would have worked to the advantage of Labour, the politics of the treaty went on to dominate Irish public life for several generations. The Labour Party, a party of the left but not strictly socialist today, has never been able to increase substantially the seventeen seats it won in 1922. The 29th Dáil, elected in May 2002, had just 20 Labour members in a 166-member house.

Constitutional Nationalism and the New Ireland

In important respects, then, the Irish state has fallen short of the vision of those who gave their lives in 1916. They were utopians and would probably not have sacrificed themselves for what Ireland was actually to become. But recognizing the revolution as unfinished ought not blind us to the significant achievements of the Irish state. It is not a Gaelic, united, or socialist Ireland, but it is an independent, democratic republic, and a welfare state. It survived the terrible days of the civil war without degenerating into the counterrevolutionary tyranny of the French and Russian revolutions. Instead, the independent Irish state has always had the support of a large majority of its people, and it has been a rare example in the history of twentieth century postimperialism of a stable and democratic new state. It is ironic that this achievement owes a great deal to the constitutional nationalist tradition which Sinn Fein thought it had destroyed in the Easter Rising and the general election of 1918.

There are a number of explanations for Ireland's political stability. Brian Farrell, for example, argues that because Ireland was already a comparatively modern society, the political upheaval from 1916 to

1923 was not accompanied by a destabilizing social revolution that would have placed unbearable strains on the new political system. He also suggests that the Roman Catholic Church was a stabilizing influence. It had always endorsed constitutionalism against revolution, and it threw its weight behind the new state in 1922.[10]

Farrell identifies two other important factors, both political, which contributed to Ireland's successful transition to self-government. He argues that the Irish Free State absorbed the modern political forms and values of British politics. It did not have to search for a new model of government. In 1919 Dáil Éireann adopted the British system of cabinet government and modeled its parliamentary procedures on those used in Parliament at Westminster, in London. Farrell writes, "There was never any serious dispute; a familiar and acceptable model —the Westminster model—was available and was simply taken over."[11] Ireland even improved on the British model by writing what in Britain are constitutional conventions, or nonlegal rules, about the powers of the head of state and the formation of the government into constitutional law for the first time in the British Commonwealth.

Farrell also argues that the Easter Rising should be viewed not as a beginning but as an episode in Irish constitutional development. The Rising was, of course, an extraordinary symbol for the new Ireland, but we can best explain the stability of the Irish state if we recognize that the constitutional tradition, which dominated Irish nationalism until 1916, reasserted itself in the Irish Free State after 1922. This is confirmed by studies of the transfer of power from the United Kingdom to the Irish Free State in 1922. Irish home rulers, constitutional nationalists all, had already been appointed by Liberal governments to control about half of the Irish civil service and judiciary by 1914 so that, in an administrative sense, the home rule state was virtually in position, awaiting only the formal transfer of power from London to Dublin. Lawrence McBride describes the response of Irish judges and civil servants to the Irish Free State eight years later:

> When given the choice, in 1922, of either serving the Irish
> Free State, which was to be established in Southern Ireland,
> or the Unionist government, which was already established
> in Northeast Ulster, the overwhelming majority (at least 80%)

of the highest ranking judicial and civil service officials chose to serve in the South. Most of these officials were the same men who had been willing to serve under the more moderate Nationalists in 1914.[12]

Ironically, many of those who chose not to serve the south went north to provide the core of the Northern Irish public service when it was created in 1921. Both parts of Ireland also benefited from the fact that the Irish civil service had been thoroughly reorganized in 1920 by Sir Warren Fisher, the Permanent Secretary to the British Treasury.

In several respects, then, the Irish Free State owed a great deal to the efforts of constitutional nationalism, although this has not been widely acknowledged in Ireland since independence. This absence of recognition is understandable, perhaps, because independent Ireland was governed by those who rejected constitutional nationalism from 1916 to 1922, but in practice they returned very quickly to it at independence.

THE EASTER RISING AND THE IRISH IMAGINATION

Constitutional nationalism provided the bases of the political practices and administration of the new Irish state, but revolutionary nationalism captured the Irish imagination. This was because the sometime revolutionaries who came to power in 1922 had no interest in admitting John Redmond and his kind to the company of Irish revolutionary heroes such as Tone, Emmet, Pearse, Connolly and the rest. The revolutionary tradition also captured the imagination of Irish writers who transmitted it to their readers. F. X. Martin writes that the Rising was planned "with exceptional military incompetence," but there was a deliberate theatrical element which was, he says, "imaginatively planned with artistic vision. . . ."[13] The purpose of the Rising was to stir the Irish nation with an extraordinary display of self-sacrifice and heroism, and in this it succeeded. As we saw in Chapter 1, W. B. Yeats was captured by the image, and within a week of the event, another Irish writer, James Stephens, was moved to report, "The blood of brave men had to sanctify such a consummation if the national imagination was to be stirred to the dreadful business which is the organizing of freedom."[14] The Easter Rising and the civil war attracted a host of other writers. They were not all uncritical of revolution. Yeats, for example, can be read quite literally when he wrote in 1916, "A terrible beauty is born."[15] And the playwright, Sean O'Casey, refused to glorify revolution in his plays, *The Shadow of a Gunman* (1923), *Juno and the Paycock* (1924), and *The Plough and the Stars* (1926), but he, too, found it impossible to escape a concern with revolution and war as themes. Constitutional nationalism could attract no such attention.

No one should deny the men and women of 1916 their place in the Irish imagination, and it would be churlish to deny the authentic pathos of Patrick Pearse's poem, "The Mother," which he composed for his own mother while awaiting execution:

> I do not grudge them: Lord, I do not grudge
> My two strong sons that I have seen go out
> To break their strength and die, they and a few,
> In bloody protest for a glorious thing.
> They shall be spoken of among their people,
> The generations shall remember them,
> And call them blessed;
> But I will speak their names to my own heart
> In the long nights;
> The little names that were familiar once
> Round my dead hearth.
> Lord, thou art hard on mothers:
> We suffer in their coming and their going;
> And tho' I grudge them not, I weary, weary
> Of the long sorrow—And yet I have my joy:
> My sons were faithful, and they fought.[16]

We might ask, however, if the romantic view of violence in the struggle for Irish freedom that Pearse presents, his "bloody protest for a glorious thing," has been entirely beneficial. It can be argued that there is a line to be drawn between respect for the sacrifices of those who gave their lives for Irish freedom on the one hand, and a cult of revolutionary violence which has no respect for liberal democracy on the other. This cult can be seen in two activities: the continuation of revolutionary activity by a small number of republicans, and the widespread use of the theme of patriotic violence in popular ballads and folklore.

Revolutionaries continue to draw inspiration and justification from the Easter Rising and the Irish revolutionary tradition. As we saw in Chapter 9, in his eulogy in 1915 at the grave of the Fenian, O'Donovan Rossa, Pearse said of the English, "They . . . have left us our Fenian dead, and while Ireland holds these graves, Ireland unfree shall never be at peace."[17] For republican extremists today, Ireland is still unfree as we enter the twenty-first century, and the Fenian dead include not only those who fell between 1916 and 1923 but those who have died in Northern Ireland since 1970, including ten republican hunger strikers, Bobby Sands and nine others, who died in Northern Ireland prisons in 1980 and 1981.

In 1873 the Irish Republican Brotherhood constitution was amended to read, "The IRB shall await the decisions of the Irish Nation as expressed by a majority of the Irish people, as to the fit hour of inaugurating a war against England. . . ."[18] The rebels of 1916 did not wait for that majority decision, but this is not unusual. Revolutionaries never do wait. They seize the day. The Easter Rising was the work of what F. X. Martin called "a minority of a minority of the minority."[19] There is no doubt that in the next several years this minority won the respect of a majority of the Irish nationalist community, as was confirmed in several general elections when revolutionaries swept the board between 1918 and 1921. But the support for the revolutionaries at that time was an anomaly in modern Irish history, and since 1922 revolutionary nationalism has been rejected by Irish nationalists literally dozens of times in elections.

In the south of Ireland, Arthur Griffith and Michael Collins, whose republican credentials were absolutely impeccable, turned to constitutionalism in 1921, after the Anglo-Irish Treaty, and began the process of separating a twenty-six-county Ireland completely from Britain. Even Eamon de Valera came to accept the constitutional framework of the new state in 1926, and once he formed a government in 1932 it took him only five years, within the law, to remove the Crown and write a republican constitution. This policy of constitutional gradualism has been endorsed by a clear majority of the Irish nationalist community in every general election in the south of Ireland since 1922, in the referendum that removed Articles 2 and 3 from the Irish constitution in 1998, and in elections in the nationalist community of Northern Ireland since its representatives entered the Northern Parliament in 1925. In addition, since at least 1973, governments of the Irish republic, knowing quite well that a unionist majority exists in North Ireland, have declared that the people of the north must decide for themselves, by democratic vote, whether to unite with the south. Irish governments have also worked assiduously to oppose support for the IRA in the U.S. Congress and Irish-American communities.

Despite this overwhelming support for constitutionalism in the nationalist community, every generation, including our own, has produced new recruits to continue the fight, and they have used the symbol of the Easter Rising to justify violence in their pursuit of a united Ireland. But their behavior has never been supported by nationalist voters, north or south, and it is profoundly undemocratic.

The revolutionary tradition is also alive in Irish popular culture, particularly in ballads. Irish men and women, in Ireland or abroad, who would no more join the IRA to fire a gun than rob a nun, are to be found in pubs and bars singing the glories of revolutionary violence. One popular song, *The Patriot Game*, attacks even Eamon de Valera "for shirking his part in the patriot game."[20] In a sense this cultural celebration of violence has an innocent explanation. The Irish love pubs, they love to sing, they have to have something to sing about; revolutionary patriotism is a much more enticing subject than John Redmond and the merits of the third home rule bill. Songs of violence, be their subjects 1798, 1848, 1916, the war of independence, the civil war, or the recent conflict in Northern Ireland, win by default, but they make very bad nationalist history.

The truth in Ireland is that while the men and women of 1916 are very important in the iconography of all Irish nationalists, the constitutional tradition dominates at the ballot box. Furthermore, the great majority of Irish nationalist politicians, journalists, and intellectuals have taken particular pains to distance themselves from the revolutionary tradition since the revival of violence in Northern Ireland in the late 1960s. They do not want it thought that the south is in any important sense responsible for violence in the north.

CONFLICT IN NORTHERN IRELAND

The conflict in Northern Ireland which reignited in the late 1960s, and is still not completely resolved, is what remains of the "Irish problem" that exploded in 1916. It would be useful, therefore, to end this book by asking if we can see in Northern Ireland the end of the road for the long history of Anglo-Irish conflict in which the Easter Rising was such an important part. Will the Belfast Agreement of 1998, which led to the resumption of self-government in Northern Ireland, finally bring peace to Ireland?

The present conflict in Northern Ireland has shared roots with the Easter Rising. Both had their origins in the existence of two communities, or ethnies, in Ireland, one nationalist and one unionist, which have very different values and aspirations. But the proximate cause for the more recent round of violence lies less in ancient ethnic hatreds than in the bad relations between the two communities in Northern Ireland that have existed since the partition of Ireland in 1921. More particularly, it lies in the abuse of the Northern Ireland political system by the unionist majority.

There is no disagreement among historians that the IRA was practically dead in Northern Ireland in 1964, or that Sinn Fein, its political wing, was moving towards constitutional activity as a neo-Marxist political party, when a nonviolent, Catholic-based civil rights movement began to agitate for an end to anti-Catholic discrimination in housing, employment, the police, and local government. The civil rights movement met violent resistance from a large number of unionists, sometimes abetted by the police, and in 1969 British troops were sent to Northern Ireland to restore order. This gave a faction of the IRA, the so-called Provisionals, an opportunity to resume the war for Irish independence that had started in 1916, with the Easter Rising. In 1970 the Provisional IRA presented itself as defender of the northern nationalist community under siege, and simultaneously it renewed its war against the United Kingdom.

When the conflict deepened in 1972, the United Kingdom Parliament abolished the Northern Ireland Parliament which had existed since 1921 and assumed direct control of the area. Since 1970 the Northern Ireland conflict has involved three states and a large number of political parties and groups who have made it much more complex than anything seen before in Ireland. Constitutional nationalism is represented by the Social and Democratic Labour party (SDLP), which was founded in 1970 by members of the civil rights movement. It has had close ties to a succession of Irish governments in Dublin and has always opposed the use of violence. In 1981, Sinn Fein, the long-time political wing of the IRA, also began to practice constitutional politics, capitalizing on nationalist sympathy for hunger strikers in Northern Ireland prisons. It had considerable success in Northern Ireland elections, and in the U.K. Parliament general election of 2001 it took more votes than the SDLP for the first time, winning four seats in Parliament to the SDLP's three. Sinn Fein takes its seats in local government and the new Northern Ireland Assembly, but not in Parliament, where its members refuse to swear the oath of allegiance to the Crown. Over time, Sinn Fein has publicly renounced violence and has been able to persuade the Provisional IRA to accept a truce and place some, at least, of its weapons beyond use. It signed the Belfast Agreement and has participated in both the new Northern Assembly and the all-party Northern Ireland Executive.

Revolutionary nationalism in Northern Ireland is represented by two paramilitary groups: the Provisional IRA and a smaller organization, the Irish National Liberation Army (INLA), which split from the IRA in 1975.

On the unionist side, constitutionalism is represented by several political parties. The largest is the Ulster Unionist party (UUP), which governed Northern Ireland from 1921 to 1972. It signed the Belfast Agreement in 1998 and since 1973 has been prepared to share executive power with nationalists, but it holds Sinn Fein responsible for IRA recalcitrance in arms decommissioning and has several times refused to cooperate with that party until progress has been made on the arms issue. A close second to the UUP in popular support is the Democratic Unionist party (DUP), founded by Iain Paisley in 1971. It is opposed to sharing power with nationalists, particularly Sinn Fein, and did not sign the Belfast Agreement.

There are two small parties associated with the two unionist paramilitary groups, the Ulster Democratic party, which is associated with the Ulster Freedom Fighters, and the Progressive Unionist party, which is associated with a smaller group, the Ulster Volunteer Force. The unionist paramilitaries have been very active through the years but it is generally accepted that their activity will cease if the Provisional IRA disarms and ceases operations.

Three states have been actively involved in the conflict. The first, of course, is the United Kingdom. It is the sovereign power in Northern Ireland, a fact that is accepted by unionists without question, and by the SDLP as an unavoidable reality, but Sinn Fein has only barely shifted from regarding Britain as an illegitimate occupying power to a negotiating partner.

Since 1972, when the U.K. Parliament abolished the Northern Ireland Parliament, the policy of successive British governments has been to establish some form of self-government in Northern Ireland that would recognize the right of nationalists to participate not only in the legislature, as they did before 1972, but in the government too. This concept, called "power-sharing," was the basis of the Anglo-Irish Sunningdale agreement of 1973 that led to a new Northern Ireland Assembly, and a power-sharing government, with both unionist and nationalist members. That political system was destroyed by unionist opposition in 1974, but the principle of power-sharing between unionists and nationalists was at the core of the Belfast Agreement of April 1998 and the new constitution for Northern Ireland that it ushered in.

The Irish Republic is the second state involved in the conflict. When Northern Ireland self-government was abandoned in 1972, work immediately began on an alternative model that would not allow unionists to monopolize political power. The Irish government was accepted as an interested party, a stakeholder, in this process. Britain knew that Irish cooperation on the border was necessary to contain the Provisional IRA, and it also believed the Irish government could help win nationalist support in the north for a negotiated settlement. The Irish government therefore participated in the Sunningdale conference of 1973 and every round of negotiations until the Belfast Agreement of 1998.

The United States is the third state involved in Northern Ireland. In the 1980 U.S. census 43.7 million Americans identified themselves as having Irish origins, and nationalist supporters are important voters in a large number of congressional districts. This is why Congress has shown considerable support for Irish nationalism over the years. But presidents conduct American foreign policy, not Congress, and they have said little or nothing in public about Ireland until 1977, although often urging an Irish settlement on British governments in private. This policy of public presidential neutrality changed in 1977.

When the conflict in Northern Ireland was at its worst, in the 1970s, some leading Irish-American politicians took sides against Britain because they took the violence to be a continuation of Ireland's long struggle for independence. Irish governments, which have always seen the IRA as a dangerous terrorist organization, persuaded the Americans not to endorse the IRA and four Irish-American politicians became particularly important in a campaign led by the Irish government to undermine the extensive IRA support network in the U.S.A.: Sen. Edward Kennedy, Sen. Daniel Moynihan, House of Representatives Speaker Thomas "Tip" O'Neill, and Governor Hugh Carey of New York. They persuaded President Carter to issue an appeal for a negotiated peace in Northern Ireland in 1977 and to support an International Fund for Ireland, which supplied economic development aid to both sides of the border.

In 1994 President Clinton became more heavily involved in Ireland's troubles than any of his predecessors. He allowed Gerry Adams, the Sinn Fein leader, to travel to the United States to meet White House officials. This was very much against the advice of the British government, but it gave Adams leverage with those in the IRA who were resisting a cease-fire. He could argue that his constitutional activities were paying dividends. Clinton also sent a special envoy, former senator George Mitchell, to prepare a report on the problem of disarming paramilitary organizations in the north and then to chair the talks which culminated in the Belfast Agreement of 1998. Clinton himself spent many hours on the telephone urging a settlement on the several negotiators, and he visited Northern Ireland in 1995 and again in 1998, after the Belfast Agreement, to encourage the peace process. His involvement in Ireland was unprecedented, and very high risk, given the possibilities for failure.

A SETTLEMENT: THE END OF THE ROAD?

Between 1967 and 1997, 3,585 people died in the Northern Ireland conflict and more than 40,000 were injured, in a population of only 1.5 million. The peak years of violence were from 1971 to 1976, but it took until 1998 to arrive at what might prove to be a viable settlement. The Belfast Agreement of 1998 bears the hallmarks of the Sunningdale Agreement of 1973, particularly a power-sharing government, an assembly elected by proportional representation, and an all-Ireland consultative body, in this case a North-South Ministerial Council. There were differences between the two agreements, of course, but the similarities remain remarkable. We might ask, therefore, what made the Belfast Agreement succeed, to date at least, and the Sunningdale Agreement fail within a few months? The answer is that there were major changes in the way the Irish problem was treated between 1973 and 1998 without which there would have been no settlement, and these changes provide a basis for some optimism about the future.

There were actually two Northern Ireland questions to be solved, and therefore two negotiations tracks, which very much complicated the peace process for many years. These tracks only came together in 1994. One question was how to reintroduce a form of self-government that would provide a role for nationalists in the government of the north. This question grew out of the civil rights movement and the allegation that unionists had used their monopoly in government to allow discrimination against Catholics. The other question was how to win the war against the IRA and the INLA, and their unionist paramilitary counterparts. This question grew out of the decision by the IRA to renew the war of independence in 1970. These were distinct questions, but unionists linked them. They were unhappy, and for most of the period unwilling, to share power with nationalists until there was peace with the IRA. It was not until 1994 that the issues of self-government and peace were linked because that year the IRA agreed to end, or at least suspend indefinitely, its war against Britain so that Sinn Fein could enter the peace talks.

Between 1973 and 1998 there were also important changes in the Irish Republic. In the early 1970s influential people in the south began to acknowledge that any solution to the Northern Ireland problem had to respect both nationalist and unionist interests, and political unification could only take place with the consent of a majority of the people of the north. This position was accepted by the Irish government at Sunningdale in 1973, but it took time to permeate through the Irish political culture, and the Irish Republic's constitutional claim to the north was only abandoned in 1998.

In the intervening years the Irish Republic changed quite remarkably as a society. Its entry into the European Union marked a transformation from a rather defensive and insular culture in the early 1950s to a cosmopolitan and European one twenty years later. In addition, the north and south found themselves converging in the sense that both were becoming more secular. In the south divorce and contraception are now permitted, most books can be read, and since 1972 the constitution has no longer given even the appearance of privileging the Catholic Church. In addition, southerners have become much more aware of the views of unionists in the north. Since the celebrations of the fiftieth anniversary of the Easter Rising (1966), governments and media in the Irish republic have toned down their tributes to revolutionary nationalism, in large part for fear of being thought to promote in some way the Provisional IRA campaign in the north. Indeed, a contributor to a book published on the seventy-fifth anniversary of the Easter Rising in 1991 called the memorial celebration at the Dublin GPO "a brief, sheepish ceremony. . . ."[21]

Changes in the United Kingdom's approach to Northern Ireland also contributed to a settlement. Between 1916 and 1967 the U.K. governments allowed the unionists a virtual veto over constitutional change in Northern Ireland, but the civil rights movement caused them to recognize the evidence of discrimination against the nationalist community that had long been ignored. Labour Prime Minister Harold Wilson (1964–70) began to apply pressure for change in Northern Ireland, and as a result, over several years, all forms of discrimination were eliminated by law. Furthermore, at Sunningdale Conservative Prime Minister Edward Heath (1970–74) guaranteed the SDLP that nationalists would have a role in any Northern Ireland government. In the Anglo-Irish Agreement of 1985, Conservative Prime Minister Margaret Thatcher (1979–90) agreed to hold regular intergovernmental conferences in Belfast and Dublin where the Irish government could make representations on behalf of the nationalists in the north. Finally, Conservative Prime Minister John Major (1990–97) agreed to accept a united Ireland if that were to be the wish of a majority in the north. It was clear from all these developments that the unionist veto had gone.

Meanwhile, the position of the unionist majority in the north also changed to recognize new political realities. As early as 1973, a significant number of Ulster Unionist Party politicians accepted the principle of a power-sharing government, although there was insufficient unionist support to make the system viable at the time, and it collapsed in 1974. However, most unionists came to accept the legitimacy of the nationalists' separate identity, and in 1998, albeit by a very narrow majority, they accepted the Belfast Agreement and power sharing. In one respect, however, the unionist position was reinforced in these years because the British and Irish governments affirmed in three formal agreements that there would be no Irish unification without the consent of a majority in the North.

The position of the nationalist minority in Northern Ireland has changed as well. As a result of the civil rights movement and the reforms that followed, nationalists were guaranteed legal equality in Northern Ireland in every aspect of their lives. Furthermore, since Sunningdale, they have been assured a share in government.

The position of Sinn Fein/IRA has also changed. The paramilitary campaign that the Provisional IRA launched against Britain in 1970 failed to force a British withdrawal, and from 1981 the revolutionary nationalists decided to wage war on two fronts. The IRA paramilitary campaign continued but Sinn Fein entered constitutional politics as a radical, left-wing nationalist party, focusing on issues of social justice and welfare. Its electoral successes in nationalist areas soon posed a threat to the SDLP, and it was this that led Britain and Ireland to sign the Anglo-Irish Agreement of 1985, which provided for Irish government participation in the intergovernmental conferences. This agreement took the wind out of the sails of Sinn Fein/IRA and its leaders appear to have decided that the paramilitary campaign would end if Sinn Fein could enter talks on the future government of Northern Ireland as a legitimate negotiating partner. The Anglo-Irish Declaration

of 1993 welcomed Sinn Fein into the peace process if it would permanently end its support for IRA violence. The IRA did not declare a cease-
fire until August 31, 1994, but when it did, Sinn Fein was allowed to
enter the peace process formally. The IRA resumed terrorist bombings
in 1996 but Sinn Fein's leaders remained committed to negotiations,
and in time they were able to win the debate over a cease-fire inside
the republican movement. Sinn Fein signed the Belfast Agreement in
1998, and the Provisional IRA has begun to disarm.

The last change in the constellation of factors influencing peace in
Northern Ireland is one we have already discussed. It was the unprecedented intervention of the United States government that helped tip
the balance in both communities in favor of a settlement.

A conference on a permanent settlement began in September 1997,
chaired by George Mitchell, who made it clear that this might well be
the last chance for a negotiated settlement of what remained of the
Irish problem. He clarified issues, kept all the parties, some of whom
refused to talk directly to each other, round the table for months of
talks, and in the end set a deadline for a settlement of Easter 1998. On
Good Friday, April 10, 1998, the Belfast Agreement was signed by the
British and Irish governments and all but one of the Northern Ireland
parties, the DUP.

The Belfast Agreement provided formal recognition of the two traditions in Northern Ireland and affirmed that the people of the north
alone will decide when and if to join a united Ireland. The British and
Irish governments agreed to implement a decision to unite, if one is
made, but at the moment there is a unionist majority in the north and
the border will remain for the foreseeable future. The agreement was
approved by a referendum in Northern Ireland, but a sign of trouble
to come was that whereas an estimated 95 percent or more of nationalists approved, only a bare majority of unionists, probably no more
than 53 percent, agreed. If the agreement is to succeed, there can be no
slippage in unionist support.

The agreement was implemented by the United Kingdom Parliament in the Northern Ireland Act of 1998, and by complementary
legislation in the Irish Parliament. The Northern Ireland Act is long,
multilayered, and complex, and as a constitution it really satisfied no
one completely because it had to be acceptable to everyone round the

table, many of whom were more interested in protecting their interests than in creating a truly viable political system. Whether it can end the long cycle of violence in Ireland is therefore problematic.

The act created a 108-member Assembly, elected by proportional representation, with domestic jurisdiction over most matters in Northern Ireland. Assembly members are required to declare themselves to be unionists, nationalists, or "other," and this process of declaration is very important because the most important votes in the Assembly require majorities from both communities. Most importantly, the Executive Committee, the government of Northern Ireland, is led by a first minister and deputy first minister, who must be elected jointly with the support not only of a majority of the Assembly but also a majority of each of the unionist and nationalist members. The effect of this rule is that one of the two leaders will always represent the unionist community and the other will always represent the nationalist community.

The act further provides that if either of the two leaders resigns, the whole executive must be dismissed and a new one be found from the Assembly. If that cannot be done, a general election must be called. The effect of this rule is that either leader can destroy the executive by resigning, and given that they will represent the largest party in each community, it is unlikely that they can be replaced by others from the Assembly, even after an election, if they resign. Direct rule from London is the only alternative. In its first three years, the Northern Ireland Executive was suspended twice because one of the two leaders, David Trimble, the unionist first minister, or Seamus Mallon, the nationalist deputy, threatened to withdraw. As this is being written, in the fall of 2002, a third suspension is in effect because of Trimble's threat to resign.

The requirement in the Northern Ireland Act that there be two leaders of government, from opposing parties and communities, either of whom can destroy the government by resigning, is a constitutional oddity, to say the least, but so too is the rest of the government. Northern Ireland government ministers are elected by the Assembly by proportional representation in a system designed to ensure that all major parties will be represented in the government, no matter how incompatible they may be. For example, four parties were represented in the first government, as this book was being written, including the Democratic Unionist party, with two ministers. The DUP rejected the Belfast Agreement and is officially committed to destroying power-sharing. Most chief executives, whether prime ministers or presidents, have at least a significant say in the appointment of a government, but in Northern Ireland, the first and deputy first ministers have to work with what they are given and there is no collective responsibility.

A similar power-sharing principle applies in the Assembly itself where the chairs of Assembly committees are elected by proportional representation so that, again, every major party has a share of power, no matter how its policies may differ from those of the Assembly as a whole, or from the government. In addition, the Northern Ireland Act requires that there be "cross community support" for certain measures approved by the Assembly, which means either the support of a majority of the Assembly and a majority of both nationalists and unionists, or the support of 60 percent of all members and at least 40 percent of each side. Any thirty members, just 28 percent, of the Assembly can request that a vote be made subject to this rule of cross community support so it can fairly easily be invoked to apply to any issue that arouses intense partisanship.

The issue that caused greatest difficulty for the Assembly from its beginning was the disarming, or decommissioning, of paramilitary groups, which the Belfast Agreement calls for. At times, unionists refused to work with Sinn Fein because they blamed it for not securing the disarmament of the IRA, which was very slow to comply. In reply, nationalists accused unionists of refusing to acknowledge that progress was being made and of using the issue to destroy the agreement. As this is being written, the decommissioning issue is slowly being resolved but other issues that strain political consensus will take its place, because the Assembly must deal with important issues in health, housing, economic development, education, social welfare, and the like that ordinarily divide political parties in every democratic political system. But given the present rules on Assembly votes, the Northern Ireland political system can only work if politicians manage to avoid partisan divisions. This means asking politicians not to act politically. In other democracies difficult decisions are made by majority votes, but in Northern Ireland the voting rules of power sharing make decisionmaking much more difficult.

There is a huge incentive to make the new Northern Ireland political system work because, as mentioned, if it fails the United Kingdom will resume direct rule, which very few people in Britain or Ireland want. Making the system work will not be easy because the central problem of Northern Ireland's self-government, the presence of two antagonistic ethnic communities, is etched deeply into a constitution that requires politicians who distrust, dislike, and sometimes hate each other to govern by consensus.

In early November 2001 the Assembly nearly collapsed when a new leadership team of David Trimble, UUP, and Mark Durkan, the new SDLP leader, narrowly failed to be elected. Although they had the support of more than 70 percent of Assembly members, they failed to win the support of a majority of Assembly unionists. Because a majority of both communities have to support the leaders, an act of constitutional trickery had to be invoked to save the day. Two "other" members declared themselves to be unionists for the day in order to vote, and then returned to being "others" again. This gave the leadership team a majority. David Ford, the leader of the centrist Alliance party, which had reluctantly contributed one of the unionists-for-a-day, was appalled by the process. He declared, "I utterly reject the notion that we are to be forever regarded as two tribes in an uneasy truce rather than a united community that cherishes true diversity."[22] The truth of the matter, however, is that the constitution was expressly written to accommodate "two tribes in an uneasy truce." This was the only arrangement acceptable to the major parties to the Belfast Agreement because it provided protections, and therefore vetoes, to both communities. Power-sharing was viewed optimistically as a way of forcing politicians to consider the interests of the whole community in their decisions, but it could as easily render the new constitution unworkable in time because of the opportunities it provides for obstruction.

For several periods, Northern Ireland self-government worked. The Assembly made law and ministers from four parties ran departments, even if the two DUP ministers opposed power-sharing. The system is suspended now. However, all but a few extremists have accepted constitutionalism as a way of political life, and if this continues the revolutionary tradition in Ireland may have been put to rest at last. But all is not perfect. Political violence has not completely disappeared, the paramilitaries have not completely disarmed, tensions flare too often between the two communities, and the constitution is fragile. It has only survived because secretaries of state for Northern Ireland have suspended the Assembly to give them time to resolve political crises, rather than abolish it.

The changes in Irish society, north and south, and in the attitudes of the major actors that were identified above, clearly indicate that the Ireland of today is a world apart from 1916, and even from 1970, and that is cause for optimism. But if progress is to continue several things will have to happen.

Any substantial paramilitary violence has to stop permanently. The system can tolerate sporadic terrorism by known fringe groups, but not another war involving the IRA, unionist paramilitaries, and the army. No democratic political system can survive if political parties are believed to be willing to return to violence if they do not always get their way constitutionally.

The politicians of Northern Ireland also have to show that they can make a very difficult constitution work. For the moment this requires that they subdue ordinary democratic political instincts and try to resolve important issues by consensus. If they can do this, at least for a while, they may be able to develop enough confidence in each other to amend the power-sharing and qualified voting provisions of the constitution in ways that will make the system less fragile.

Finally, the people of Northern Ireland will have to support political parties that are committed to making the system work. In this regard there were ominous signs of movement away from the moderate center in the 2001 United Kingdom general election. On the unionist side, because Sinn Fein was thought not have done enough to disarm the IRA, there was a significant movement of unionist voters away from the relatively moderate Ulster Unionist party towards the more extreme Democratic Unionist party, which opposes power-sharing. On the nationalist side, for the first time, Sinn Fein out-polled the SDLP in a general election.

If this movement towards the extremes of unionist and nationalist politics continues, so that the DUP and Sinn Fein become the largest parties in their communities, power-sharing in Northern Ireland
will be destroyed because the DUP will not work with Sinn Fein. If
that happens, there will almost certainly be a return to violence, and
to the revolutionary tradition of the Easter Rising. For the moment,
then, the future of Northern Ireland is in the hands of voters.

1 Patrick Pearse, *The Best of Pearse*, Proinsias MacAonghusa and Liam Ó Réagáin, eds.
   (Cork, 1967), p. 133.
2 Quoted by Foster, p. 196.
3 Gareth W. Dunleavy, *Douglas Hyde* (Lewisburg, 1974), p. 38.
4 Garret FitzGerald, *Towards a New Ireland* (Dublin, 1972), p. 12.
5 Quoted in Clare O'Halloran, *Partition and the Limits of Irish Nationalism* (Dublin,
   1987), 102–103.
6 O'Brien, p. 121.
7 Terence Brown, *Ireland: A Social and Cultural, History, 1922–79* (London, 1981),
   p. 131.
8 Beckett, p. 151.
9 Brian Farrell, *The Founding of Dáil Éireann* (Dublin, 1971), p. 87, and Patrick Lynch,
   "The Social Revolution that Never Was," in Williams, pp. 45–47.
10 Farrell, pp. xv–xx.
11 Ibid., p. xviii. See also Ward, *Irish Constitutional Tradition*, pp. 167–295.
12 Lawrence W. McBride, "The Transformation of the Irish Bureaucracy, 1892–1914,"
   unpublished paper, 1978, p. 16.
13 Martin, p. 9.
14 Stephens, p. 11.
15 Yeats, p. 205.
16 Pearse, p. 192.
17 Pearse, p. 134.
18 Kevin B. Nowlan, "Tom Clarke, MacDermott, and the I.R.B.," in F. X. Martin,
   Leaders and Men of the Easter Rising: Dublin 1916 (Ithaca, New York), p. 110.
19 Martin, "1916—Myth, Fact and Mystery," p. 108.
20 Charles Carlton, ed., *Bigotry and Blood* (Chicago, 1977), p. 107.
21 Declan Kiberd, "The Elephant of Revolutionary Forgetfulness," in Máirín Ní
   Dhonnchadha and Theo Dorgan, eds., *Revising the Rising* (Derry, 1991), 1.
22 *Irish Times*, October 22, 2001.

Bibliography

The books discussed below provide only an introduction to Irish history and the Easter Rising but many of them contain bibliographies that will help the reader to explore topics in greater detail.

GENERAL SURVEYS OF IRISH HISTORY

Beginning students will find Robert Kee, *Ireland: A History* (Boston, 1982) useful. More experienced readers should turn to R. F. Foster, *Modern Ireland: 1600–1972* (New York, 1988); L. M. Cullen, *The Emergence of Modern Ireland, 1600–1900* (London, 1981); and A. Jackson, *Ireland 1798–1998: Politics and War* (Oxford, 1999). The most comprehensive study of the constitutional evolution of Ireland, north and south, is A. J. Ward, *The Irish Constitutional Tradition: Responsible Government and Modern Ireland, 1782–1992* (Washington, 1994). Conflict in Ireland is considered in T. Bartlett and K. Jeffery, eds., *A Military History of Ireland* (New York, 1996) and M. Marcus, *Ireland's Holy Wars: the Struggle for a Nation's Soul, 1500–2000* (New Haven, CT, 2001).

IRELAND TO THE UNION, 1801

The New History of Ireland series includes A. Cosgrave, ed., *A New History of Ireland—Volume II: Medieval Ireland 1169–1534* (Oxford, 1993); T. W. Moody, F. X. Martin, and F. J. Byrne, eds., *A New History of Ireland—Volume III: Early Modern Ireland 1534–1691* (Oxford, 1991); and

T. W. Moody and W. E. Vaughan, eds., *A New History of Ireland—Volume IV: Eighteenth-Century Ireland, 1691–1800* (Oxford, 1986). Nicholas Canny, *Making Ireland British, 1580–1650* (Oxford, 2001) describes the conquest of Ireland, which is also the subject of R. D. Edwards, *Ireland in the Age of the Tudors* (New York, 1977). M. Wall, *The Penal Laws, 1691–1760*, 2d ed. (Dundalk, 1967), is an important work on the Penal Laws. British-Irish relations before the union are reviewed in E. M. Johnston, *Great Britain and Ireland, 1760–1800* (Edinburgh, 1963) and *Ireland in the Eighteenth Century* (1974). R. E. Burns, *Irish Parliamentary Politics in the Eighteenth Century* (Washington, DC, 2 vols., 1989–1990) examines the Irish parliament at its height, and the period of the Act of Union is the subject of G. C. Bolton, *The Passing of the Act of Union* (Oxford, 1966); P. M. Geoghegan, *The Irish Act of Union: A Study in High Politics, 1778–1801* (New York, 1999); and G. O'Brien, *Anglo-Irish Politics in the Age of Grattan and Pitt* (Dublin, 1987).

Surveys of Ireland from the Union, 1801

Two volumes of the New History of Ireland deal with the period from the union to partition. See W. E. Vaughan, ed., *New History of Ireland—Volume V: Ireland under the Union, I: 1801–1870* (Oxford, 1989) and *A New History of Ireland—Volume VI: Ireland Under the Union, II: 1870–1921* (Oxford, 1996). F. S. L. Lyons, *Ireland Since the Famine* (London, 1973) is a balanced treatment of Irish history since the mid-nineteenth century. J. J. Lee, *The Modernization of Irish Society, 1848–1918* (Dublin, 1973) is shorter and more provocative. Other short surveys suitable for students include D. G. Boyce, *Ireland, 1828–1923: From Ascendancy to Democracy* (Oxford, 1992); K. T. Hoppen, *Ireland Since 1800: Conflict and Conformity* (New York, 1998); T. Hachey, *Britain and Irish Separatism: From the Fenians to the Free State, 1867–1922* (Washington, DC, 1984); L. McCaffrey, *Ireland: From Colony to Nation-State* (Englewood Cliffs, NJ, 1977); O. Walsh, *Ireland's Independence, 1880–1923* (London, 2002); and Patrick O'Farrell, *England and Ireland Since 1800* (New York, 1975). B. Girvin, *From Union to Union: the Act of Union to the European Union* (Dublin, 2002) is a very recent account of modern Ireland. J. J. Lee, *Ireland: 1912–1985* (Cambridge, 1989), and Dermot Keogh, *Twentieth-Century Ireland: Nation and State* (Dublin, 1994) are major studies of the twentieth century.

SPECIAL TOPICS FROM THE UNION TO 1923

Nationalism

General studies of Irish nationalism include S. Cronin, *Irish Nationalism: A History of its Roots and Ideology* (New York, 1981); M. Ward, *Unmanageable Revolutionaries: Women and Irish Nationalism* (London, 1983); and J. Mac Laughlin, *Reimagining the Nation-State: The Contested Terrains of Nation-Building* (Sterling, VA, 2001), a postmodern analysis. J. H. Murphy, *Abject Loyalty: Nationalism and Monarchy During the Reign of Queen Victoria* (Washington, DC, 2001) considers Irish loyalty to the Crown in a period of intense Irish nationalism.

Constitutional Nationalism

Daniel O'Connell and his campaigns for Catholic emancipation and repeal are the subjects of many books, notably a definitive two volume biography, O. MacDonagh, *The Hereditary Bondsman: Daniel O'Connell, 1775–1829* (London, 1988), and *The Emancipist: Daniel O'Connell, 1830–1847* (London, 1989).

The home-rule period is usefully studied through biographies, including D. Thornley, *Isaac Butt and Home Rule* (Westport, CT, 1976); F. S. L. Lyons, *Charles Stewart Parnell* (New York, 1977), a definitive Parnell biography; and R. Kee, *The Laurel and the Ivy: the Story of Charles Stewart Parnell and Irish Nationalism* (New York, 1993). P. Bew, *Parnell* (Dublin, 1980) is a convenient short biography. F. S. L. Lyons, *John Dillon* (Chicago, 1968) is a fine study of one of Parnell's successors, but John Redmond is neglected. D. Gwynn, *The Life of John Redmond* (Freeport, NY, 1971), though useful, is dated, as is F. S. L. Lyons, *The Irish Parliamentary Party, 1890–1910* (Westport, CT, 1975), a study of the Irish party after Parnell. Studies of British politicians who influenced home rule include J. Loughlin, *Gladstone, Home Rule and the Ulster Question, 1882–1893* (Atlantic Highlands, NJ, 1987); Roy Jenkins, *Asquith* (New York, 1967); R. Blake, *Unrepentant Tory* (New York, 1956), a study of the Conservative leader, Bonar Law; and C. Shannon, *Arthur J. Balfour and Ireland, 1874–1922* (Washington, DC, 1988).

K. T. Hoppen, *Elections, Politics, and Society in Ireland, 1832–1885* (Oxford, 1984) sets the electoral context for Irish politics before home rule. L. McCaffrey, *Irish Federalism in the 1870s: A Study in Conservative Nationalism* (Philadelphia, 1962) considers the early home-rule movement. Parnell's role is skillfully presented in Alan O'Day, *The English Face of Irish Nationalism: Parnellite Involvement in British Politics, 1880– 1886* (Niagara Falls, NY, 1977). He also wrote *Irish Home Rule, 1867– 1921* (New York, 1998). P. Jalland, *The Liberals and Ireland: The Ulster Question in British Politics to 1914* (New York, 1980) focuses on Ulster. L. W. McBride, *The Greening of Dublin Castle* (Washington, 1991) is an excellent and original study of the influence of constitutional nationalism on the Irish administration before independence. T. Garvin, *The Evolution of Irish Nationalist Politics* (Dublin, 1981) discusses continuities in pre- and post-independence Irish politics, and J. Kendle, *Ireland and the Federal Solution: The Debates over the United Kingdom Constitution 1870–1921* (Kingston, ONT, 1989) considers Ireland in a study of UK federal proposals.

Romantic Nationalism

A good account of nineteenth-century romantic nationalism is still Malcolm Brown, *The Politics of Irish Literature: From Thomas Davis to W. B. Yeats* (Seattle, 1972); a blend of literary and historical analysis. The Young Ireland movement is considered in R. Davis, *The Young Ireland Movement* (Totowa, NJ, 1987), and Brendan O'Cathaoir, *John Blake Dillon: Young Irelander* (Dublin, 1990). The founder of the Gaelic League is the subject of J. E. Dunleavy and G. Dunleavy, *Douglas Hyde: A Maker of Modern Ireland* (Los Angeles, 1991). Brian Walker, *Dancing to History's Tune: History, Myth, and Politics in Ireland* (Belfast, 1996) focuses on Northern Ireland.

Revolutionary Nationalism

N. Curtin, *The United Irishmen: Popular Politics in Ulster and Dublin, 1791–1798* (Oxford, 1994), reviews the United Irish movement of the 1790s, and M. Elliott, *Wolfe Tone: Prophet of Independence* (New Haven, 1989) is a definitive study of its leader. L. O'Broin, *Revolutionary Underground: The Story of the Irish Republican Brotherhood, 1858–1924* (Totowa, NJ, 1976) and *Fenian Fever: An Anglo-American Dilemma* (New York, 1971) both focus on Fenianism. T. Garvin, *Nationalist Revolutionaries in Ireland, 1858–1928* (Oxford, 1987) reviews revolutionary nationalism during its most active phase. Biographies of Fenians include

D. Ryan, *The Fenian Chief* (Coral Gables, FL, 1967), a study of James Stephens, and *The Phoenix Flame* (London, 1937), a study of John Devoy. M. Bourke, *John O'Leary: A Study in Irish Separatism* (Athens, GA, 1968,) considers the IRB leader.

Irish Unionism

Studies of unionism include D. W. Miller, *Queen's Rebels: Ulster Loyalism in Historical Perspective* (New York, 1978); A. T. Q. Stewart, *The Ulster Crisis* (London, 1967), by an Ulster historian; and P. Buckland, *Irish Unionism 1: The Anglo-Irish and the New Ireland, 1885–1922* (New York, 1973), a study of Southern Unionists; and P. Buckland, *Irish Unionism 2: Ulster Unionism and the Origins of Northern Ireland, 1886–1922* (New York, 1973), a companion volume on Northern unionists. A. Jackson, *The Ulster Party: Irish Unionism in the House of Commons, 1884–1911* (Oxford, 1989) considers early unionism in Parliament and J. F. Harbison, *The Ulster Unionist Party, 1882–1973* (Belfast, 1973) brings the Ulster Unionist party into the 1970s. E. Marjoribanks and I. Colvin, *The Life of Lord Carson*, 3 vols. (London, 1932, 1934, 1936), is still a useful study of the Ulster Unionist leader. Conservative unionism is the subject of L. P. Curtis, Jr., *Coercion and Conciliation in Ireland, 1880–1892* (Princeton, NJ, 1963); and J. Smith, *The Tories and Ireland: Conservative Party Politics and the Home Rule Crisis, 1910–1914* (Portland, OR, 2000).

Irish Americans

D. N. Doyle, *Ireland, Irishmen and Revolutionary America* (Dublin, 1981) considers early Irish activity in America. Pioneering studies include T. N. Brown, *Irish-American Nationalism* (Philadelphia, 1966), and L. McCaffrey, *The Irish Diaspora in America* (Bloomington, IN, 1976). Kerby Miller, *Emigrants and Exiles: Ireland and the Irish Exodus to North America* (New York, 1985), is a prize-winning book on the mindset of Irish immigrants. K. Kevin, *The American Irish: A History* (New York, 2000) is a recent study. The impact of the Irish question on Anglo-American relations is considered by J. O'Grady, *Irish-Americans and Anglo-American Relations, 1880–1888* (New York, 1976); A. J. Ward, *Ireland and Anglo-American Relations, 1899–1921* (Toronto, 1978);

and F. M. Carroll, *American Opinion and the Irish Question, 1910–1923* (New York, 1978). A broad study of Irish emigration, including to America, is D. Fitzpatrick, *Irish Emigration, 1801–1921* (Dundalk, 1984).

The Great Famine

For many years the most popular book on the Great Famine was C. Woodham-Smith, *The Great Hunger* (New York, 1963). J. Donnelly, *The Great Irish Potato Famine* (Phoenix Mill, Gloucestershire, U.K., 2001) may become the new standard. J. Mokyr, *Why Ireland Starved: A Quantitative and Analytical History of the Irish Economy, 1800–1850* (London, 1983) is a sophisticated quantitative analysis. See also C. Kinealy, *The Great Irish Famine: Impact, Ideology, and Rebellion* (New York, 2002); P. Gray, *The Irish Famine* (New York, 1995); C. O'Grada, *The Great Irish Famine* (New York, 1995); and Peter Gray, *Famine, Land, and Politics: British Government and Irish Society, 1843–1850* (Dublin, 1999).

Irish Churches

Studies of the churches in modern Ireland include several works by S. J. Connolly, including, *Religion, Law, and Power: The Making of Protestant Ireland, 1660–1760* (Oxford, 1992), *Religion and Society in Nineteenth-Century Ireland* (Dundalk, 1985), and *Priests and People in Pre-Famine Ireland, 1780–1845*, 2d ed. (Dublin, 2001). See also E. R. Norman, *The Catholic Church and Ireland in the Age of Rebellion* (Ithaca, NY, 1965) and an impressive body of work based on church archives by E. Larkin, *The Roman Catholic Church and the Emergence of the Modern Irish Political System, 1874–1875* (Washington, DC, 1996); *The Roman Catholic Church and the Creation of the Modern Irish State, 1876–1886* (Philadelphia, 1975); *The Roman Catholic Church and the Plan of Campaign in Ireland, 1886–1888* (Cork, 1978); and *The Roman Catholic Church in Ireland and the Fall of Parnell, 1888–1891* (Chapel Hill, 1979). See also D. W. Miller, *Church, State and Nation in Ireland, 1898–1921* (Pittsburgh, 1973), and D. Akenson, *The Church of Ireland: Ecclesiastical Reform and Revolution, 1800–1885* (New Haven, 1971).

The Land Question

The land question is the subject of important studies by J. Donnelly, *Landlord and Tenant in Nineteenth Century Ireland* (Dublin, 1973), and

The Land and the People of Nineteenth Century Cork: The Rural Economy and the Land Question (Boston, 1975); B. L. Solow, *The Land Question and the Irish Economy, 1870–1903* (Cambridge, MA, 1971); P. Bew, *Land and the National Question in Ireland, 1858–82* (Atlantic Highlands, NJ, 1979); and S. Clark and J. Donnelly, *Irish Peasants: Violence and Political Unrest, 1780–1914*. W. E. Vaughan, *Landlords and Tenants in Mid-Victorian Ireland* (Oxford, 1994) indicates that land issues were not always violent. T. W. Moody, *Michael Davitt and Irish Revolution, 1846–82* (New York, 1981) is a biography of the leader of the Land League.

The Easter Rising, 1916

A good introduction to people involved in the Easter Rising is F. X. Martin, ed., *Leaders and Men of the Easter Rising, Dublin, 1916* (Ithaca, NY, 1967). Patrick Pearse is the subject of an excellent biography, R. D. Edwards, *Patrick Pearse: The Triumph of Failure* (London, 1977). Edwards also authored *James Connolly* (Dublin, 1981). See also C. Desmond Greaves, *The Life and Times of James Connolly* (New York, 1971) by a Marxist historian; and S. Levenson, *James Connolly: A Biography* (London, 1973). The labor movement as a whole is thoroughly surveyed in A. Mitchel, *Labour in Irish Politics, 1890–1930* (New York, 1974). Sinn Fein is considered in Padraic Colum, *Arthur Griffith* (Dublin, 1959) and Richard Davis, *Arthur Griffith and the Non-Violent Sinn Fein* (Dublin, 1974), a study of Sinn Fein before the Rising. Eoin MacNeill, the ambivalent leader of the Irish Volunteers, is the subject of F. X. Martin and F. J. Byrne, eds., *The Scholar Revolutionary: Eoin MacNeill, 1867–1945* (Dublin, 1973). Eamon de Valera is the subject of many studies including an official biography, Lord Longford and T. P. O'Neill, *Eamon de Valera* (Boston, 1971). Roger Casement's controversial life is the subject of B. Inglis, *Roger Casement* (New York, 1974). Countess Markievicz has two biographers, J. Van Voris, *Constance de Markievicz* (Old Westbury, NY, 1972), and A. Marreco, *The Rebel Countess* (Philadelphia, 1967).

F. X. Martin used the years surrounding the fiftieth anniversary of the Easter Rising to open up serious academic study of the event. See F. X. Martin, *The Irish Volunteers, 1913–1915* (Dublin 1963); *The Howth Gun-Running, 1914* (Dublin, 1964); and his two superb journal articles, "1916—Myth, Fact and Mystery," *Studia Hibernica* (Dublin, 1967) and "The 1916 Rising—A Coup d'Etat or a Bloody Protest?" *Studia Hibernica* (Dublin, 1968). The most detailed account of the Rising is probably M. Caulfield, *The Easter Rebellion* (Westport, CT, 1975), based in part on interviews with survivors. Other useful books include C. Duff, *Six Days to Shake an Empire* (South Brunswick, NJ, 1967); R. McHugh, ed., *Dublin, 1916* (London, 1976); O. D. Edwards and F. Pyle, eds., *The Easter Rising* (London, 1968); D. Ryan, *The Rising* (Dublin, 1966); and R. Fitzgerald, *Cry Blood, Cry Erin* (New York, 1966). J. Stephens, *The Insurrection in Dublin* (Chicago, 1965) reprints Stephens's eyewitness account of the Rising first published within weeks of the event. L. O Broin, *Dublin Castle and the 1916 Rising* (New York, 1971) describes the Rising from the perspective of the British administration in Dublin.

The Irish War of Independence, the Founding of the Irish Free State, and the Irish Civil War

E. Purdon, *The War of Independence* (Cork, 2001) is a very brief account of the war, which is also described in a number of biographies of Michael Collins, including, U. O'Connor, *Michael Collins and the Troubles: The Struggle for Irish Freedom, 1912–1922* (New York, 1996); T. R. Dwyer, *Big Fellow, Long Fellow: A Joint Biography of Collins and De Valera* (Dublin, 1998); R. Taylor, *Michael Collins* (London, 1970); T. P. Coogan, *Michael Collins: The Man Who Made Ireland* (Boulder, CO, 1996); and V. MacDowell, *Michael Collins and the Irish Republican Brotherhood* (Dublin, 1997). C. Younger, *A State of Disunion: Arthur Griffith, Michael Collins, James Craig, Eamon de Valera* (London, 1972) considers leaders on both sides of the conflict. Lord Longford and T. P. O'Neill, *Eamon de Valera* (London, 1970) is the official biography of de Valera. The British role is described in D. G. Boyce, *Englishmen and Irish Troubles* (Cambridge, MA, 1972), and C. Townshend, *The British Campaign in Ireland, 1919–1921* (New York, 1975), a fine account drawn primarily from British military records. Studies of the processes leading to the Anglo-Irish Treaty of 1921 include J. M. Curran, *The Birth of the Irish Free State, 1921–1923* (University, AL, 1980); T. Garvin, *1922, The Birth of Irish Democracy* (New York, 1996); Lord Longford, *Peace by Ordeal* (London, 1972); and T. Hennessey, *Dividing Ireland: World War I and Partition* (New York, 1981). M. Hopkinson, *Green Against Green: the Irish Civil War* (Dublin, 1988), is a good study of the Irish Civil War, 1921–23. See also Arthur Mitchell, *Revolutionary Government in Ireland: Dáil Éireann, 1919–22* (Dublin, 1995).

IRELAND SINCE 1923, NORTH AND SOUTH

Northern Ireland

D. Birrell and A. Murie, *Policy and Government in Northern Ireland: Lessons of Devolution* (Dublin, 1980) describe the government of Northern Ireland from 1921 to 1972. T. Hennessey, *A History of Northern Ireland, 1920–1996* (New York, 1997) continues into the period of "the long war." See also P. Buckland, *A History of Northern Ireland* (Dublin, 1981) and M. Farrell, *The Orange State* (London, 1976).

The Northern Ireland "troubles" since the 1960s are the subject of an enormous literature. For very useful interpretations see J. Whyte, *Interpreting Northern Ireland,* (Oxford, 1991); J. McGarry and B. O'Leary, *Explaining Northern Ireland: Broken Images* (Oxford, 1995); and P. Dixon, *Northern Ireland: The Politics of War and Peace* (New York, 2001). See also P. Bew and G. Gillespie, *Northern Ireland: A Chronology of the Troubles, 1968–99* (Dublin, 1999); T. P. Coogan, *The Troubles: Ireland's Ordeal 1966–1996 and the Search for Peace* (Boulder, CO, 1996); and M. Mulholland, *The Longest War: Northern Ireland's Troubled History* (New York, 2002). For the IRA see B. O'Brien, *The Long War: The IRA and Sinn Féin* (Syracuse, NY, 1999); M. L. R. Smith, *Fighting for Ireland? The Military Strategy of the Irish Republican Movement* (New York, 1995); and J. B. Bell, *The IRA, 1968–2000: Analysis of a Secret Army* (Portland, OR, 2000). For the uncertain future of the Belfast Agreement of 1998 see R. Wilford, ed., *Aspects of the Belfast Agreement* (Oxford, 2001). C. O'Clery, *Daring Diplomacy: Clinton's Secret Search for Peace in Ireland* (Boulder, CO, 1997) reviews the first part of President Clinton's intervention in Northern Ireland. A. J. Wilson, *Irish America and the Ulster Conflict, 1968–1995* (Washington, DC, 1995) explores grass roots Irish-American interest in Northern Ireland.

Independent Ireland

R. Fanning, *Independent Ireland* (Dublin, 1983) is a short survey of the south since independence. T. Brown, *Ireland: A Social and Cultural History, 1922 to the Present* (Ithaca, 1985) is a unique blend of historical and literary scholarship. The influence of the constitutional and parliamentary traditions is the subject of B. Farrell, *The Founding of Dail Eireann: Parliament and Nation Building* (Dublin, 1971), and B. Farrell, ed., *The Irish Parliamentary Tradition* (New York, 1973). The role of the IRA and its influence in post-independence Ireland is considered in two books, J. B. Bell, *The Secret Army: The I.R.A., 1916–1974* (Cambridge, MA, 1970); and T. P. Coogan, *The I.R.A.* (London, 1970). R. Dunphy, *The Making of Fianna Fáil Power in Ireland, 1923–1948* (Oxford, 1995) examines the dominant political party in modern Ireland. Ireland's role in redefining the British empire is skillfully described in D. H. Harkness, *The Restless Dominion: The Irish Free State and the British Commonwealth of Nations, 1921–31* (New York, 1970). Anglo-Irish relations are also considered in P. Canning, *British Policy Towards Ireland 1921–1941* (Oxford, 1985); D. McMahon, *Republicans and Imperialists: Anglo-Irish Relations in the 1930s* (New Haven, 1984); and B. Sexton, *Ireland and the Crown, 1922–1936* (Dublin, 1989). C. O'Halloran, *Partition and the Limits of Irish Nationalism: An Ideology Under Stress* (Atlantic Highlands, NJ, 1987) describes how Ireland's policies undermined its claim to the north after independence. J. Whyte, *Church and State in Modern Ireland, 1923–1979* (Totowa, NJ, 1980) discusses the role of the church in modern Ireland.

Index

The Easter Rising: Revolution and Irish Nationalism, Second Edition
Developmental editor: Andrew J. Davidson
Copy editor and production editor: Lucy Herz
Proofreader: Claudia Siler
Printer: Strategic Content Imaging